A Redneck Bites the Big Apple

A REDNECK BITES THE BIG APPLE

BO WHALEY

Rutledge Hill Press
Nashville, Tennessee

Published in Nashville, Tennessee, by Rutledge Hill Press, 211 Seventh Avenue North, Nashville, Tennessee 37219

Distributed in Canada by H. B. Fenn & Company, Ltd., 1090 Lorimar Drive, Mississauga, Ontario L5S 1R7

Typography by E. T. Lowe, Inc., Nashville, Tennessee

ISBN 1-55853-363-X

Printed in the United States of America

1 2 3 4 5 6 7—99 98 97 96 95

To Joe, the son every father prays for;
the husband every wife dreams of;
the father every child could respect;
the brother any sister would be proud to have.
In Joe, I am well pleased.

CONTENTS

INTRODUCTION

THIS BOOK HAS BEEN ON THE TIPS OF MY fingers for forty years, twenty-two years before I typed the first word of the first of thirty-three hundred newspaper columns I've written since 1978. I didn't know how or when but I felt certain that I would write about the day I stepped off the bus and walked out of the Port Authority Bus Terminal and stood at the corner of 40th St. and 8th Ave., Thanksgiving Eve 1954.

The concrete, steel, and asphalt giant that is New York City almost took my breath away. That's understandable considering that I was born in a little Georgia town, Scott, that boasts a population of less than two hundred. Being the son of a Methodist preacher, I was raised in seven other South Georgia towns, the largest with a population of twenty-five hundred. So on my first visit to the Big Apple it is understandable that New York City flat scared me to death by its size alone.

I hadn't been in New York more than twenty-four hours when I knew I would return. I knew I had to because it is a fascinating city. I spent only four days there on my maiden visit and that's like eating only one potato chip. I saw and went places I had only read about. I watched the city wake up and put its wheels in motion. I heard it moan and groan like a sleepy school kid on a cold and rainy Monday morning; like a giant luxury liner preparing to put out to sea; or the passenger train that would take me back to Washington from whence I came getting ready to pull out of Pennsylvania Station. Finally, awakened and ready, the city was well underway with millions manning their individual stations to set the business and industry in motion. It became a beehive of activity and I tried to watch every bee. The taxi fleets fascinated me with their constant honking and yelling, but getting nowhere. Riding in a cab for the first time was an experience I would not soon forget. I felt like a mouse crawling through a maze of cats. I was convinced I'd never survive. But my driver kept repeating in broken English, "You be okay, okay?"

I inhaled as much of the city as possible during my four-day visit. I saw a Broadway play, stood on top of the Empire State Building on 34th Street and surveyed the skyscrapers, the little cars and midgets scurrying about. Everybody seemed to be ten minutes late for whatever it was they were rushing to. I ate a great hot dog from a 42nd Street pushcart, a slice of coconut pie from one of the world's great inventions . . . the automat where you win a prize every time you deposit money, the best hot pastrami and potato salad in the world at a delicatessen, the first I'd ever seen, and a steak that made my mouth water in Greenwich Village at a place called Don

Stampler's Steak Joint. I know I would have another one day, and I did.

The train to Washington pulled out of Pennsylvania Station two days later. I was on it. But I knew I would return. I wasn't through with New York City yet.

Ten years later, in 1964, I returned for a six-year stint as an FBI agent. I lived in New Jersey and commuted like millions of others. Funny thing about New York and New Jersey. People who live in New York City never say they're going to New Jersey. They simply say, "See you'se guys later. I'm goin' over to Joisey." The "New" is a wasted word, never used. On the other hand, people who live in New Jersey never say they're going to New York. They simply say, "Gotta' go into the city. Be back later." Nobody asks, "What city? Washington? Baltimore? Philadelphia? Boston? New Haven?" It's not necessary. Everybody knows when you say you're going into the city that you're talking about New York.

I observed New Yorkers closely during my six years there. They are a unique breed. I made no notes before writing this book. The memories I have of New York are sufficient. The way they talk (and they really do talk funny), the way they work, the way they play is fascinating. It's like watching a movie live on its streets and in its neighborhoods. They are opinionated, and authoritative—especially on sports. You'd think each one lived in the basement of Madison Square Garden or in the dugout at Yankee Stadium.

So, what is this book about? It is about New York and its people as seen through the eyes of a South

Georgia boy. It is about the great friends I made there. New York is a very special place, still a little scary but special just the same. There aren't enough adjectives to describe it. No writer could adequately describe it. No painter could adequately portray it. No photographer could adequately capture it on film. You have to feel it, you have to smell it, you have to hear it to really know it.

What is New York? Say what you will about the tall buildings, the financial district, the garment district, Hell's Kitchen, the Bowery, Brooklyn, Harlem, Yonkers, Times Square, and the Bronx. New York is people, millions of people, trying to make their way in the entrails of a giant and survive every day. One day at a time. Love it or hate it, New York is special.

A Redneck
Bites the
Big Apple

YES, VIRGINIA, THERE IS LIFE WEST OF THE HUDSON RIVER

NO DOUBT THE ONE THING THAT AMAZED about New York City when I moved there in 1962 was the total lack of knowledge by many of its residents that life existed outside its borders. For them, life ended at the Hudson River and everything west of it was barren and unpopulated. As far as they were concerned, Atlanta was just the other side of the Brooklyn Bridge where grits were grown and harvested; Dallas was one big oil well; Miami was just off the coast of Spain, near a place called Cuba, where their rich neighbors spent the winters and returned home in June with a great suntan; and California was an island somewhere out in the Pacific

Ocean where movie actors and rock musicians hung out until needed for a movie part or a rock concert in Madison Square Garden. New Jersey was a suburb of New York and there was no such place as Arkansas. Just a bad dream or the figment of somebody's imagination.

Of course, we have a similar situation down here in Atlanta. People who live there are convinced that civilization ends in Marietta, and north and south Georgia are where the rejects end up. The people in south Georgia are convinced that there ain't nothing north of Waycross, and their counterparts in north Georgia will swear there's nothing south of Dalton.

I am a good example. I was born and raised in little bitty towns all over south Georgia and was out of high school before I realized that there was life north of Macon and south of Valdosta. That's when I heard about Nashville, Tennessee, and had it preached to me for years that if a person lived a good life, did right by the Lord, ate his grits regularly, and paid his child support on time, when he died he went to the Grand Ole Opry. If not, he went to the Metropolitan Opera.

The advent of two things in America in the past forty-five years have served to change the thinking of both northerners and southerners concerning the makeup of America: World War II and television.

World War II no doubt did more to educate those of us north and south, east and west, to the ways of other people in other regions of America than any other single event in this century. Indeed, New Yorkers learned that there was life west of the Hudson River.

New Yorkers were grabbed up, drafted, and sent to the boondocks for basic training in such places as Camp Blanding, Florida, Camp Wheeler, Georgia, Fort Benning, Georgia, Fort Jackson, South Carolina, Fort Stewart, Georgia, Fort McLellan, Alabama, Fort Riley, Kansas, Fort Sill, Oklahoma, Fort Hood, Texas, Fort Bragg, North Carolina, and a hundred others. They were forced to learn a new language (southern), adapt to a new environment (humid), eat new foods (grits), and learn new customs (manners). It wasn't easy, but they did it. Many found the southern belles to their liking, married them, and homesteaded in the promised land after the war. Many are still here. Ours, here in the South, was a way of life they never knew existed—until the war sent them to us.

Many were away from New York for the first time in their lives. Some were born in New York and never got more than a few blocks from their homes in Brooklyn, the Bronx, Queens, Manhattan, and Staten Island. World War II was indeed an eye opener to those sent from the Big Apple to peach country.

Likewise for those of us who were sons of the south when Uncle Sam wrote and said, "Greetings. You have been selected . . ."

World War II was indeed a war, but on the home front it provided an education for so many of us who were not well traveled. We saw countrysides and lifestyles that we never dreamed existed. Then, in the early fifties, television burst into our living rooms with is cameras taking us to places we had only seen in movie houses on "Movietone

News." Now we saw how the other half lived, not only in America, but world wide. Did World War II and television make us more understanding and tolerant of those who live in faraway places? I sure hope so.

My First—and
Last—Subway Ride

THE FIRST NEW YORK SUBWAY I EVER SAW I rode on. That was forty-two years ago, on Thanksgiving Day 1954. It was also the last subway I ever rode on, and I have no plans of ever riding the subway again.

I boarded the subway car after much pushing and shoving by the people behind me. I dropped my tokens on the floor, and my hat fell off. What a subway debut. "If my friends could see me now," I thought.

It didn't take me long to decide that women are better than men at boarding subways. I know, because I received at least one spiked heel in the shin and more than one knee in the groin during the process of boarding that infernal train. And I learned the hard way that "excuse me" is not proper subway etiquette. "Move it" is more like it.

What really shook me up was when I looked down and saw a man sprawled out on the floor in the rear of the train car. He did not appear to be resting. Instead, he appeared to be dead. Dried blood covered his face and head. No one was paying any attention to him. In fact, one passenger was standing on his left hand.

At the next stop, and only the good Lord knows where we were, I hustled to the front of the train and inquired of a man I now know was the motorman, who runs the train, if he was aware that there was a dead man on the floor in the third car back.

"Well I'll be darned," he said.

"Shouldn't we do something?"

"Like what?" he demanded. "Do I look like an undertaker to you?"

"But the man is dead. Don't you understand?"

"So he's got less troubles. All aboard now!"

It was hopeless—for the dead guy and for me. So I didn't get back on the train. Instead, I walked outside the station and hailed a cab. As I rode back to my hotel, the Taft, I mentioned the man in the subway car to the cab driver, who spoke very little English—and not much more Spanish, supposedly his native tongue.

"Dead, you say? Only one?"

That was that. I may be from the South, but I know when to surrender. The folks back home in Georgia wouldn't believe it, I thought, that you could ride around town with a dead guy right next to you without causing a commotion or lifting a finger to help. Back in my hotel room, I tried not to get depressed over the sad state of affairs in the Big Apple. Instead, my thoughts turned homeward, to a little old lady in Atlanta.

The woman was standing in the pouring rain waiting for a bus. When the bus finally arrived at the stop, she slowly made her way on board, with a long line of would-be passengers behind her. After much fumbling in her purse, she pulled out a folded, wrinkled twenty-dollar bill, which she handed to the bus driver. He sighed out loud and counted her change. The woman dropped the change. The she proceeded to slowly and methodically pick up her coins from the floor, one by one. With her change in hand, she began to deposit the fare. "Thank goodness," whispered one hopeful rider.

Little did the old lady know that she was ever so carefully dropping her coins—nickel by nickel, dime by dime—into an air-conditioning vent. She apologized as she tried to retrieve them. But, of course, she couldn't. Then she turned and saw all the people behind her, dripping wet as they waited to board. She started to speak, but instead, she dropped her purse, spilling all the contents. While on her hands and knees gathering her belongings, she spoke to those in line: "Please excuse me. I've never ridden one of these buses before."

"Well I can tell you, lady," said one man, "We sure ain't missed you."

As I prepared to leave my hotel room and once again venture forth into the wilds of New York, I felt some empathy for that woman. We were two of a kind—confused in Atlanta and concerned in New York. I can only trust that the lady made it to her destination, but to this day I wonder whether my dead friend is still riding the subway car.

A Tree Lights up
in Brooklyn

For years and years there has been a continuing discussion regarding a communication gap between the North and the South. Up there, they think we talk funny, and down here, we *know* they do. Many times the meaning is lost in the translation. Other times you just had to be there.

For example, I've never quite understood why New Yorkers continue to misuse the words *oil* and *Earl*. If I stop at a service station in the Bronx, fill my tank, and ask to have my oil checked, the owner will no doubt say to his assistant, Earl, "Hey, Oil! Check this guy's earl, would ya'?"

On the other hand, a fella' from the Bronx makes a pit stop in Georgia on his way to Florida and hears the station owner say, "Ya'll come back rail soon, ya' heah? I 'prechate ya'll stoppin' by. I'll just be runnin' along now 'cause I got to get the missus and carry her to th' doctor."

Who could blame the guy from the Bronx for thinking the man is on his way to pick up his wife, sling her across his back, and tote her to the doctor's office? The northern visitor has every right to be confused, as did I one cold day in Brooklyn in 1962.

Since that fateful December day when I first drove a car in New York, I have vowed to drive in the Big Apple on only two occasions—when I'm chasing somebody, or when somebody's chasing me. If traffic laws were enforced in the city every cab driver would be in jail, instead of out roaming the streets, driving like maniacs and scaring the heck out of the rest of us. Drive from Manhattan to Brooklyn without getting side-swiped or rear-ended and you're a genius.

I had received a message to meet another FBI agent in front of an address on Remsen Street, just off Flatbush Avenue, in Brooklyn at 5:00 P.M. Do you know what 5:00 P.M. in Brooklyn means? That's just about the time all the mental patients from Bellevue Hospital break out, steal cars, and go for joy rides—straight down Flatbush Avenue. There's another name for it, of course—rush hour.

It was raining when I exited the Holland Tunnel on the New York side and made my way to Flatbush Avenue. Naturally I made a wrong turn and ended up on Atlantic Avenue. But that's no surprise. Those who know me well will tell you that I could have easily gotten lost in the Holland Tunnel itself. I maneuvered my way through rush hour traffic as best I could in search of Remsen Street. It was nearing 5:00 and I didn't have a clue as to where I was or where I needed to be. Read a map, you say? No way. I can't read a map for the life of me. Had I tried that I would have no doubt ended up back in the Holland Tunnel, or at Yankee Stadium.

I did find Flatbush Avenue again, however, and stayed on it until I came to a policeman directing traffic in the rain at Flatbush and Utica, apparently not too happy about it. I looked at my watch. It was 4:50 P.M. I pulled ahead and rolled down my window.

"Excuse me, sir. Can you direct me to Remsen Street?"

"Straight ahead, tree lights up. Move along now," he said.

Within minutes I was back, with my window down once again.

"Excuse me, sir. But can you direct me to Remsen Street?" I spoke even slower than usual, thinking the policeman hadn't understood me the first time.

"Straight ahead, tree lights up," he said, with just a touch of antagonism in his voice.

Wouldn't you know it? Quick as a wink I was back again. This time, the policeman recognized me.

"You again?" he snarled.

"Yes sir," I offered. "I tried twice but I didn't see any tree."

"Tree? What tree?" came his response.

"The tree you said lights up."

"Look, buster. I said tree lights up. You know, one, two, tree. Whassamattayou? Can't you count? Now gedouddaheah."

Sure enough, I went three lights up and there it was, as big as life—Remsen Street. And not a tree in sight.

GRITS 101

I HAVE ASSIGNED MYSELF AN ALMOST IM-possible task here, trying to describe grits to a pair of New Yorkers. Describing grits to New Yorkers is as hard as describing a trombone without using your hands. In teaching this class I have to approach the subject matter assuming that my students have little, if any, knowledge of grits. This is understand-able as there are many other southern delicacies with which they are not familiar.

This course is being offered based on a true-to-life experience I had with a husband and wife, from the Big Apple, who stopped in my hometown of Dublin, Georgia, to have breakfast on their way to Florida.

The establishment they chose to eat in is an authentic, homemade biscuit, down-home cooking, grits-
served-with-all-meals, cafe. It was established by
Ma Hawkins in 1931. She operated it until her death
and then her daughter, Grace Lord, took it over. She
operated it until shortly before her death, and then
her son, Jimmy Lord, assumed ownership in 1979
and is the present owner.

I am as much a fixture at Ma Hawkins Restaurant
as are the coffeemaker, the iced tea urn, the cracklin'
bread, and Dot and Eddie Mae, the absolute mon-
archs of the kitchen. They perform magic there
every day with their culinary masterpieces. Nobody
does it better. I eat there more than one thousand
times a year, and when I am out of town I think
about it. Here's precisely what happened:

I could hardly believe my ears on a Saturday
morning as I sat in Ma Hawkins Restaurant, having
breakfast. It was as if a bolt of lightning had struck
when I heard a woman sitting two booths away ask
the waitress, Liz, "What are grits? Can you describe them?"

"Jus' a minute, ma'am," Liz told her and turned to
walk to my booth.

"Bo, will you do me a favor?"

"What's that?"

"Will you please go up there and tell that woman
in th' third booth what grits are? She ain't frum
raoun heah, I don't think," Liz explained.

I've always welcomed a challenge, so I agreed to
try. I cleared my throat to make way for my best
Rhett Butler accent before walking to the third
booth, occupied by a man and a woman.

"Howdy, folks," I began. "Haow y'all this fine mawnin'?"

"Hoi," said the woman, and I knew right off that I had a pair of sho 'nough Yankees on my hands.

"An' jus' haow kin ah be uv suvvice to y'all?" I asked, pulling up a chair from a nearby table.

"We're on our way to Florida and this is our first time in the South," the woman began.

"Ah see. An' jus' wheahbouts might y'all be frum?"

"New York City."

"Well welcome to Dixie."

Holding the menu in her hand, she pointed to an item and said, "It says here that something called grits is served with each breakfast order and . . ."

"Tha's right, ma'am. An' a whole heap o' dinnuh an' suppuh awduhs, too. No exter charge f'r th' greeitz. They're sort of, uh . . . a bonus, ah reckon ya' might say," I explained.

"What are grits?" she asked. "Are they anything like Cream of Wheat?" As a true son of the South, I was insulted, but I didn't let on.

"Oh, no, ma'am! They ain't nothin' lak Cream o' Wheat," I assured her. "Ya' see, ma'am, daoun heah we figger that don't nobody 'cept sick people an' sissies eat Cream o' Wheat. Baout th' only place ya' kin git it is at th' hospital an' nursin' home."

"Please tell me more about grits," she pleaded. "I'd love to be able to tell my friends back in New York about them."

I cleared my throat again and went at it.

"Well, it's lak this, ma'am. Greeitz is corn ground up in a special way in a grist mill, an' tha's a mill used f'r grindin' grain. An' corn is grain. A feller kin do a bunch o' things with corn. He kin feed his hawgs, make corn likker tha's sometimes called moonshine or white lightnin', or take it to th' grist mill an' have it groun' into greeitz," I explained.

"I see," she said. "But what do grits look like?"

"They look a whole lot like dandruff, an' taste 'baout like dandruff, too, 'less'n ya' doctor 'em up a little," I explained. "Greeitz, lak cottage cheese, need a little help. Butter helps. So does red-eye gravy."

"Red-eye gravy?"

"Yes, ma'am. Tha's gravy whut comes from fryin' country ham. Rail good on homemade cathead biscuits, too. You see, the very main reason folks up Nawth don't lak greeitz is that nobody evah showed 'em haow t' fix 'em."

"And do you eat grits?" she asked, frowning.

"Evah day o' my life, ma'am."

"I'm fascinated. Please tell me more about grits," she begged.

"Awright. Naow, ya' gotta' 'memver that they's two kinds o' greeitz. Lak gasoline comes reg'lar an' unleaded, greeitz comes reg'lar an' instant. But jus' f'rget the instant an' go with th' reg'lar, ya' heah? Don't mess aroun' with no instant greeitz. Daown heah tha's worse 'en havin' a run in y'r stockin', goin' t' church with y'r slip showin', or eatin' pumpernickel bread."

"Do they serve instant grits here, in this restaurant?'

"Lord, no! Don't let Jimmy Lord, th' owner, or Dot and Eddie Mae in th' kitchen hear ya' say that!"

"Why not?"

"'Cause I can't stand the sound of loud hollern' an' screamin', tha's why," I said. "Accusin' Ma

Hawkins of servin' instant greeitz would be worse'n accusin' Rush Limbaugh uv bein' a lib'ral."

"And you people down here don't eat Cream of Wheat or hash brown potatoes for breakfast? Just grits. Why?" she asked.

"Well, it's lak this, ma'am. Daown heah we feel that breakfus' without greeitz is lak a road sign without bullet holes. It just ain't southern."

ROBBIE NELL BELL

TASTES THE

BIG APPLE

I'VE VISITED NEW YORK PROBABLY TWENTY-five times since moving back home to Georgia in 1965. I always have a good time, no matter when I go, but the Christmas season is special. New Yorkers firmly believe that Christmas is theirs alone, like World Series time used to be in the 1950s and 1960s when the New York Yankees dominated baseball and the Yankee players were household names. Easter, with its bonnets, is also a special time in New York, as is New Year's. But Halloween 1986 is my most memorable time ever in the city, for several reasons.

My first book, *Rednecks and Other Bonafide Americans*, had been released just three weeks earlier, and I had fully recovered from a heart attack and my doctor had given me permission to live. I thought that was real nice of him. He also gave me permission to visit his office, and pay him on a regular basis. I balked, but after reconsidering, I concluded that I would rather make regular visits and pay him than make a lone visit and a lump sum payment to the undertaker. It wasn't really a hard decision to make.

Accompanying me on my trip to New York was Robbie Nell Bell, from Alma, Georgia, one of my favorite people and the main character in *Rednecks and Other Bonafide Americans*. She's a redneck, and one of the most naturally funny people I know, but not on purpose. It's just the way she is.

I must deviate here long enough to provide more specific details about Robbie Nell if this story, which is absolutely true, is to have any meaning. So let me set the record straight about Robbie Nell Bell. That's her name all right. But that ain't what you hear when she says it. It comes out "Robbie Nail Bail, fum Almer," slow and easy, like cane syrup in January.

Robbie Nell has two brothers, Fred and Jesse, whom she affectionately refers to as "Fray-ed" and "Jay-ssie." And she has an uncle in "Chicargo," an "ain't on my mommer's side in Cissy-row, Iller-noise," and several cousins scattered all over Michigan. Plus a "grandma in Minneanapolis, Manysoter." When I first met Robbie Nell she was gainfully employed as the head waitress and bouncer at Mel's Juke, about a six-pack north of Broxton, Georgia, on U.S. Highway 441. The juke-box was playing "Daddy Died, and Mama Cried, 'Cause His Insurance Had Done Lapsed." Another quarter brought on "I Stuffed Her Turkey and She Cooked My Goose," followed by "We Split the Double Wide; She Got the Inside and I Got the Outside." Her choice of songs will really bring tears to a country boy's eyes.

I was sitting at the counter reading a newspaper when I heard her ask, "Whut's it gonna be, buddy?"

"Lowenbrau," I said matter of factly.

"Don't sell no wine in heah," she said. "Jus' beer."

I settled for a longneck Bud, the house specialty, and continued reading as I sipped.

"Whut's th' news?" she asked. "Anything good?"

"Oh, I was just reading about a guy up in New York who was convicted for raping a nun, stabbing a priest, and stealing the Sunday morning collection from a Catholic church."

"Dayum! Tha's terribl'," she said. "Does it say what they give 'im?"

"Let's see," I said as I thumbed back through the paper. "Yeah, here it is. He got a total of 730 years, without parole."

"Th' SOB! They orta' giv' 'im life," Robbie Nell growled.

Robbie Nell is as country as grits, cathead biscuits, and cane syrup. If she owns a dress, I've never seen it. But the girl does for blue jeans what Dolly Parton does for sweaters.

She stands tall at 5'11" in her bare feet, a couple of inches taller when wearing her Tony Llama cowboy boots. She's slim, but eats like she's going to the electric chair and never gains an ounce. At twenty-two she's about like she was at twelve, and amazingly she's still single. Well, most of the time. She's pretty and slender, with shoulder length brown hair that frames her face, and clear blue eyes that could melt your heart (except on occasional Monday mornings when they're hangover red).

We boarded the Delta jet at the Atlanta airport shortly after noon the day before Halloween. Robbie Nell had never flown before, but you'd never have known it. She knows no fear, of anything. Working at Mel's Juke took care of that.

Our seat assignments put me on the aisle and Robbie Nell in the middle seat. A well-dressed man in his mid-fifties was already in his window seat, reading the *New Yorker* magazine. I judged from his appearance that he must have been some type of executive. He didn't speak or in any other manner acknowledge our presence. He just glanced over his half-rim reading glasses and returned his eyes to his magazine.

"Howdy," said Robbie Nell as she eased into her seat. "How you doin' today?"

"Just fine, thank you," said the man politely, but with an air of rigidity.

I knew this was going to be an interesting flight. Anything done with Robbie Nell is interesting.

She fumbled with her seat belt, and having never flown before was obviously experiencing difficulty fastening it. The man next to her noticed, put down his magazine, and asked, "Would you like me to help you with that?"

"I'd sure 'prechate it," she said, smiling.

In a matter of seconds the seat belt was secured and the plane taxied down the runway for takeoff.

"I ain't never flew none before now," she said.

"Oh, is that so?" her new friend asked. "Are you scared?"

"Nah, jus' curious."

The takeoff was smooth, and before the FASTEN SEAT BELT light was turned off Robbie Nell and her neighbor were deep in conversation.

"Whare 'bouts ya' goin'?" she asked.

"New York," he said with his first smile of the flight.

"Ya' live in New York?"

"Yes, I've always lived there."

"What kinda' work do ya' do?"

"I'm executive vice president of a Manhattan bank."

"Manhattan? Wher' 'bouts is that at?"

"It's in New York City."

Robbie Nell was impressed. She turned to me and said, "Ya' hear that? First time I ever been in an airplane and I wind up sittin' next to a vice president of a bank. Dang!"

"And what do you do, may I ask?" asked her friend.

"I'm th' waitress an' bouncer at Mel's Juke."

"Oh? And just where is Mel's?"

"Oh, it's 'bout a six-pack north o' Broxton, on 441."

The banker didn't pursue the subject. The flight attendant appeared to take our drink orders. He ordered a Scotch and water. Robbie Nell asked for "Margareter," and I settled for a Coke.

A brief silence was broken when Robbie Nell asked, "'Bout how high up you reckon we are?"

"I'd say roughly 25,000 feet, more or less."

"Uh huh. Tha's purty high, ain't it?"

"Yes, pretty high."

"I know some ol' boys back home what gets higher'n this mos' Saturday nights, an' they ain't even got no airplane."

The New Yorker laughed heartily, and then said, "I'll bet they do."

For the remainder of the flight Robbie Nell and the New Yorker talked nonstop, pausing only to laugh. She had him in the palm of her hand. Shortly, the announcement came from the cockpit that we would be landing soon at LaGuardia Airport in about ten minutes. The FASTEN SEAT BELT light came on, but there was no problem this time. Robbie Nell had never even unfastened hers.

The banker leaned forward, looked at me for the first time, and asked, "Where will you two be staying in the city?"

"We have reservations at the Milford Hotel."

"I'm familiar with it," he said. "It's on 8th Avenue near Times Square, right?"

"That's right," I said.

"How will you be getting there from the airport?"

"Oh, we'll take a taxi I guess."

"Well, the bank limousine is picking me up and I'd be pleased to have you and Robbie Nell ride in with me and I'll drop you off at the Milford."

"That's mighty nice of you," I said. "If you're sure it isn't too much trouble."

"No trouble at all. Is that all right with you, miss?"

"Shoot yeah! I've seen them big cars on TV but I ain't never rode in one."

"Well, you will shortly, young lady."

Robbie Nell withdrew momentarily into deep thought, chin in hand. Then, she said, "Can I ask you something Mr. Palmisano?"

"Sure."

"Well, don't get mad at me now, but I've always heard that folks whut live in New York are uppity and not polite. That ain't true, is it? You sure ain't like that."

"Thank you, young lady. I appreciate that," he said as he reached for her hand. "No, all New Yorkers aren't uppity and rude. You just remember that there are good people and bad people everywhere.

And I have been fortunate to meet a pair of good ones from Georgia on this flight."

Robbie Nell said nothing, but leaned to his cheek and gave him a soft kiss. He patted her head in response.

The limo ride to the hotel was nice, and a real treat for Robbie Nell. She barely spoke, for she was too busy seeing New York for the first time.

We unloaded our bags and stood on the sidewalk. Palmisano shook my hand firmly and gave Robbie Nell a kiss on the forehead. She hugged him warmly.

As the limousine pulled away from the curb, the rear window went down and Palmisano's face appeared. With a wave he yelled, "Y'all come back now, you heah?"

The next day, Robbie Nell had been up for hours when I called her room at 9:00 A.M. That didn't surprise me.

"Good morning! Are you all set for a busy day?"

"You betcha'!" she said. "I'm ready to roll."

"Have you had any breakfast?"

"Oh, yeah. 'Bout two hours ago."

"Well I'll come and get you in ten minutes and you can sit with me while I have mine. Okay?"

"Sure. Sounds good to me."

When I got to her room she had made the bed, cleaned the bathroom, and emptied the trash cans. I said nothing, realizing that this was her first time in a hotel. But I would loved to have seen the look on the housekeeper's face later in the day when she came to clean room 515.

Breakfast was pleasant. The conversation centered primarily around Mr. Palmisano and what a nice fellow he was.

"I rilly liked him," Robbie Nell allowed. "He gave me his card an' said we could call him if we wanted to 'fore we lef' town. Reckon we could?"

"Certainly. We'll do just that."

"Thanks. I would like to tell him bye."

We left the hotel and walked to Times Square. "Boy! This is a busy place, ain't it?" exclaimed Robbie Nell.

"Sure is," I responded. "One of the busiest spots in the world."

As we made our way down Broadway toward 34th Street, Robbie Nell's eyes were wide open. So was her mouth as she gazed upward to the top of the Empire State Building.

"We'll go up there later, if you want to," I said.

"I'd sure like that," she said, still gazing skyward. "Ain't no silos that high back home, is there?"

"Hardly," I said, marveling at the way her mind worked.

"How would you like to go to Macy's?"

"You mean that big store we read 'bout back home?"

"Right."

"Shoot, I reckon! I'd like to see it so I can tell Mama 'bout it. Where 'bouts is it at?"

"Oh, it's not far. We can walk from here."

Once inside Macy's, she was amazed. She didn't know where to start looking, so I guided her in the direction of the ladies department. After about thirty minutes she stopped at a counter in the lingerie section. A clerk who looked more like a mannequin than a woman was unpacking silk pajamas and stacking them on a shelf.

"Boy, them's purty!" said Robbie Nell.

The clerk hesitated before acknowledging our presence. She coldly asked us if there was something she could help us with.

"I was jus' lookin' at that stuff whut you been unpackin'," said Robbie Nell. "Sure are purty."

"They're 100 percent pure silk, and they're on sale today at 25 percent off."

"What are they?"

"Silk pajamas, for $337.50."

"What do you do with 'em?"

"They're pajamas, young lady. What do you think you do with them? You wear them at night, of course."

"Oh," said Robbie Nell. "Then I don't need none. I don't go nowhere at night much, 'ceptin' to bed."

We turned to leave and I looked over my shoulder at the clerk. She was petrified, and that suited her personality.

After Macy's, we went to the Empire State Building as promised. We went all the way to the top, 102 stories. Robbie Nell couldn't believe it.

"Kinda makes y'r skin crawl, don't it?" she said.

I agreed, and we made our way down. We walked up but took the elevator down. She could have walked both ways. You can do that when you're twenty-two. But when you're fifty-six, it makes a heck of a lot of difference.

We spent the rest of the morning at a bookstore, had lunch at Rockefeller Center while watching the ice skaters, and walked for a few minutes before catching a taxi to another store, in Queens.

"That Rockyfeller sure had a bunch o' money, didn't he?" she concluded.

"Yeah," I said. "A whole bunch."

We arrived back at out hotel around 5:00 P.M. and went straight to the lounge. It was decorated for Halloween with ghosts, skeletons, and pumpkins all around. The bar area was covered with fake spider webs. Robbie Nell ordered a Margarita. I ordered a Coke.

The bartender placed the drinks before us and asked, "Are you folks guests of the hotel?"

"Yes."

"Then the drinks are complimentary," he said.

"Thanks! I 'prechate it!" said Robbie Nell.

"Our pleasure," the bartender said.

I watched Robbie Nell as she inhaled every inch of the lounge. She didn't miss a thing. Finally, she turned to me and said, "I rilly 'prechate you bringin' me up heah t' New York. I can't wait t' git back home an' tell ever'body at Mel's 'bout it. An' I c'n tell 'em whut a real juke looks like. This heah is rilly nice. An' Mel ain't gonna b'leeve me when I tell 'im I rode in a real limousine with a vice president of a Manhattan bank. You gonna back me up?"

"All the way, Robbie Nell. And you can show Mel the guy's business card for proof."

"Right! Tha's a great idy! I might even call Mr. Palmisano fum Mel's an' let Mel talk to 'im. How 'bout them apples?"

"Right on," I said. "Now let's get some dinner."

"You know me, I'm always hungry."

I had made reservations for eight at Lindy's. I thought Robbie Nell would enjoy it, especially the cheesecake inasmuch as she's a dessert freak. She eats strawberry shortcake and lemon pie for breakfast most mornings. The dinner was excellent, as was the cheesecake. I bought one for her mama, but I doubted that it would make it all the way home. So I bought a second one just in case.

As we walked back to the hotel, it dawned on me that Robbie Nell might appreciate a real night on the town.

"Whatever you want t' do is all right with me," she said.

"Well, it's just that you're a beautiful young woman in New York City for the first time, and it's Halloween. I just don't think it would be right for you to sit in a hotel room and watch television by yourself your last night. I'd like to take you out on the town."

"Sounds great."

Back at the hotel I asked the bartender for a recommendation.

"Do you know your way around this area?" he asked.

"Yes," I answered. "I used to live here."

"Then you know how to get over to Paramus, in Joisey?"

"It's just across the George Washington Bridge, right?"

"Right. Have you got a car?"

"No, but I'll rent one."

"Okay. There's a place in Paramus called Rumors. Great club. Great music. There'll be a big crowd tonight for Halloween, and you should have a great time. Ricky, my best buddy, will be on the door. Just tell him Al sent you. He'll take good care of you."

"Thanks, I appreciate your help."

We left the hotel at 8:30 P.M. and arrived in Paramus an hour later and began cruising in search of Rumors. It didn't take us long. Robbie Nell spotted the big sign. She also spotted the banner that read, "Halloween Special—Margaritas Two for the Price of One All Night Long!"

"This is my lucky night," said Robbie Nell.

I spoke to Ricky on the way in. He waived the ten-dollar cover charge and found us a table near the band.

"Let me know if you need anything," he said.

From that point on, until we left at about 4:00 A.M., I can vouch for the fact that one little Georgia lady had herself a ball. She captured the place, downed Margaritas by the dozen, and danced the night away.

She fell asleep before we reached the George Washington Bridge, and I woke her up that afternoon about two. We had a six o'clock flight back to Atlanta. She slept the whole way. I think she could have slept clear through November. It was a night Robbie Nell will never forget. And you can bet the folks in Paramus won't either.

Not the New York I Knew

I DON'T KNOW IF THERE WAS A FULL MOON, UFOs circling overhead, or what, but I got the surprise of my life in New York in January 1990. And it was a nice surprise at that.

I was in the city to attend the retirement party in honor of a good friend with whom I'd worked for several years. He was hanging it up after thirty dedicated years of service to the FBI. I flew into the city and funny things began happening right off the bat. Everybody was being nice to me—in New York. I told my old friend George Rottenberry about it when I got back to Georgia, but he didn't believe me.

"You'll have to tell that to somebody what ain't been there, son. I been, an' I know," he said. "I spent two years in the Army at Fort Dix an' I felt like the runt o' th' litter from th' time I set foot off'n th' train till I got back home. I got kicked at, stepped on, an' made fun of ever'where I went up there. You get in New York an' ever'body acts like you dropped out in th' third grade."

Well, no matter what George thinks, I was treated real nice by everybody for three days. It's been five years now and I'm still a little shocked.

I was in the hotel coffee shop my first morning in the city, and I approached the cashier and asked if there was a newspaper rack nearby.

"What paper would you like?" she asked.

"The *New York Times*," I said.

"I have one in my office," she responded. "I'm finished with it and you're welcome to it. Just a minute. I'll get it for you."

My head was swimming. Was I in New York City or Salt Lake City?

"Here. Let me straighten it out for you. Some of the sections are out of order," she offered.

I stood and waited. She finally handed me the paper, good as new. I walked back into the coffee shop and immediately sniffed my glass of orange juice, convinced that the waiter had no doubt laced that sucker with a generous portion of Vodka.

I walked to the basement and got a shoe shine. The fella manning the brush and cloth actually started up a conversation with me. Unheard of in my days living there.

"Cold enough for you?" he asked.

"You better believe it," I said.

I walked back up for another cup of coffee in the coffee shop. It really was a cold day. In a few minutes I asked the waiter for my check.

"There's no charge, sir. I remember you. You've already been in for breakfast."

I couldn't believe my ears.

That night I was looking for a restaurant to have dinner. I had a recommendation and I caught a cab. The driver tried hard but could not find the restaurant. He apologized repeatedly, and refused a tip. It was getting to me, all this kindness. And in New York?

I approached a man on the street and asked if he knew the location of the restaurant. He politely answered in the affirmative, and added, "I'm walking that way. Come along and I'll show you."

When we reached the restaurant, the maitre d' was very pleasant, and he spoke so that I could understand him. He showed me to my table and assured me that a waiter would be with me shortly.

The restaurant was quite crowded, but in a few minutes the maitre d' returned and said, "Pardon me, sir. But if you will kindly follow me I now have a more desirable table for you. It's more private and secluded. That makes for better dining."

Dang! I was getting sick of this. Atlanta? Sure. Houston? Yes. Nashville? Absolutely. But New York?

My dinner was excellent. The service was perfect. I tipped the waiter generously and thanked the maitre d' on my way out.

Out in front of the restaurant, on the sidewalk, I

was returned to the real world of New York in a hurry. Two cab drivers were fighting, and a cop was trying to break it up.

I was tempted to say "thank you" to the two cabbies for making New York seem more like New York, but I chose to leave well enough alone.

NEW YORK TRIVIA

- State bird: Bluebird
- State flower: Rose
- State motto: *Excelsior* (Ever Upward)
- State song: "I Love New York"
- State tree: Sugar Maple

Sittin' Up with Uncle Jake

I LEARNED DURING THOSE YEARS IN NEW York that Will Rogers was right when he said, "No matter how far away from home a man may roam, what degree of success he attains, or how dismal a failure he might become—he always has an inner desire to return home one day."

During the more than four years that I worked in New York and lived in New Jersey, I was fortunate to become friends with many fine people. We were close enough that they would laugh at me and my southern ways, and I would return the good-natured ribbing by ridiculing some of their northern peculiarities.

Oh, we didn't fight the Civil War all over again, but we did reminisce about it quite frequently. They would jab me about my grits and I would throw their Cream of Wheat, a sick man's grits, right back at them. Sure, I was outnumbered, but so was the Confederate Army most of the time.

My best Yankee friend was Tony Piersante, from Brooklyn. We laughed a lot when we were with each other, and I liked that. Tony's friends joked with me about my southern heritage, but Tony would not allow them to insult me. At six-foot-six and 290 pounds, he was a good man to have around.

Tony called me at home late one Saturday afternoon. His brother-in-law, Joe Trabucco, had died that morning, and he invited me to go with him to the Trabucco home in the Bronx to pay our respects to Joe's family.

Joe, who had also been a friend of mine, had a nice wife, Maria, and seven children. Their ages ranged from three to fifteen, four boys and three girls. Maria was pretty, and an excellent cook. She prepared dishes I couldn't pronounce but had little difficulty digesting. (In her Italian household, if Maria had any doubt about the palatability of a particular dish, she just added more garlic.)

When we arrived at the Trabucco home about 10:00 P.M., I received the surprise of my life. The noise was deafening. It sounded like New Year's Eve, the Fourth of July, and Columbus Day all rolled into one. There must have been fifty people there, drinking, eating, laughing, and telling stories about Joe.

There was a bar, a bartender, a keg of beer, and tables loaded down with food, with more arriving at regular intervals. Over in a corner of the living room, quiet and sober, and stiff as a board, was Joe.

"What's going on?" I whispered to Tony.

"These are Joe's friends and relatives, honoring the memory of Joe," he explained. "It's called a wake. You mean you've never been to one?"

"Awake?" I questioned.

"Right, a wake. Most of these people will be here all night."

I glanced over at Joe, laid out in a coffin under a dim light. No doubt in my mind that ol' Joe was dead as Hillary Clinton's health care plan. Awake? No way. Asleep? You betcha'.

"Seems to me that it would more appropriately be called asleep than awake," I offered.

"Nope. It's always been called a wake. Don't you folks in Georgia sit up with the deceased the night before the funeral?"

"Sure. We call it sittin' up."

"And how is that different from a wake?"

"Well, first of all, there isn't any liquor. Also, it's a pretty solemn occasion. No jokes about the deceased. It's a pretty respectful time with lots of crying, mostly by distant relatives and businessmen to whom the deceased owed money," I explained.

"Sounds pretty dull to me," said Tony.

"It is most of the time, but not always. I remember one time in particular when excitement reigned."

"Tell me about it."

So I did.

Raymond Lofton turned thirteen a few days before the death of his uncle, Jake Lofton, who was slightly older than the Palace of Versailles at the time of his demise.

Raymond was a good boy, very obedient, who never shirked a family responsibility. So it was only natural that when his father, Luther Lofton, approached him and said he was old enough to take his turn, along with other family members, in the time-honored tradition of sittin' up with his uncle the night before the funeral, he raised no objection. But he wasn't too keen on the idea.

Raymond had always balked at being around anybody or anything dead. It was his nature. His assigned duty of sittin' up with Uncle Jake would be his initial participation in such a ritual, and although he didn't really cotton to the idea, he would do it because his daddy said he should.

At 9:00 P.M., Raymond entered the living room of the house, located near a swamp about eight miles from town. Uncle Jake was laid out in front of a window, reposing in a coffin underneath an open window. Raymond's cousin, James Barlowe, his uncle, Gus Lofton, and his daddy were seated in folding funeral home chairs, clutching hand-held cardboard funeral home fans. There was a picture of the McKibben Brothers Funeral Home on one side and an artist's conception of heaven, a lake, and Jesus on the other.

Raymond moved slowly to a folding funeral home chair, picked up the hand-held cardboard funeral home fan, and sat down, not knowing quite what to expect, or what was expected of him.

Outside, the weather was wet and unruly. Heavy rain beat on the windows and strong winds manhandled a lone, loose shutter on the living room window next to Uncle Jake's coffin, slamming the shutter roughly and repeatedly against the side of the house. Streaks of lightning sprinted across the dark sky, igniting explosive thunder that shook the house.

Uncle Jake had been injured severely in an automobile accident many years before his death, and a spinal injury had left him badly stooped. The McKibben brothers did a really fine job of running a leather strap from his heels to the back of his neck in order to straighten him up sufficiently to lay him in the coffin so the lid could be closed for the funeral. Raymond was not aware of this.

At 10:00 P.M., Raymond's daddy stood up and said, "Well boys, if y'all are gonna' sit up I b'lieve I'll go on up to bed," and left the room. That left Raymond, his Uncle Gus, and his Cousin James to sit up with Uncle Jake. They sat in relative silence, with the rain, lightning, and thunder continuing with an ever increasing tempo, until about 11:00, when Uncle Gus got up out of his folding funeral home chair, stretched, and said, "Well, if you two boys are gonna' sit up for a while I think I'll go on upstairs and get some sleep." With that, Gus was gone.

Raymond looked at James and James looked at Raymond. Both alternately looked at Uncle Jake.

Shortly thereafter, James followed Luther and Gus upstairs after saying, "Well, Raymond, if you're gonna' sit up for a while, I think I'll go on upstairs and go to bed." His departure left Raymond alone in the room with Uncle Jake.

Raymond sat motionless, holding his hand-held cardboard funeral home fan, listening to the constant ticking of the clock on the mantel. The family cat snuggled on his feet.

Suddenly, at the stroke of midnight, the rain, lightning, and thunder went crazy at the same time. It sounded like a train wreck. The rain was coming down harder than ever, repeated lightning dominated the sky, and a tremendously loud clap of thunder hit like a bomb, shaking the house from one end to the other. An oil lamp fell from the mantel, and the damaged shutter near Uncle Jake's coffin was blown off its hinges.

The cat scrambled to get underneath the sofa. A door slammed shut in the hallway. Yet Raymond, seated in his folding funeral home chair and clutching his hand-held cardboard funeral home fan, was unmoved. Then, the worst thunder of the night sounded across the sky. It shook Uncle Jake's coffin so fiercely that the leather strap running from his heels to the back of his neck snapped and Uncle Jake bolted upright in his coffin. At this point Raymond arose from his folding funeral home chair, cast down his hand-held cardboard funeral home fan, and announced in a strong and determined voice, "Well, Uncle Jake, if you're gonna' sit up I think I'll go on upstairs and go to bed." With that, Uncle Jake was left alone, sittin' up with himself.

MAKING THE GRADE

NEW YORK CITY IS A TOUGH OLD BIRD, AND unrelenting. It's every man for himself, and the weak don't make it. If unable to fend for yourself, you might as well pull up stakes and move on to greener, softer pastures. The hardness of the city has claimed many a good man. The rigor of everyday existence, and pushing and shoving to get home for the weekend, tears at the nerves.

One main problem New York City has is too dang many people in such a small area. It matters not where you want to go or what you want to do, you're going to have to stand in line and wait to do it. You decide to go to a little out-of-the-way sandwich shop for a nice quiet lunch, and what happens? You get within sighting distance and there are more people there for lunch than there are at Yankee Stadium for a doubleheader with the Red Sox.

I've often wondered how many people live in New York City by choice. I'd venture to say a small minority. Frankly, I can't see why anybody would want to live there if they didn't have to.

I'm familiar with one man who handled the New York situation very well, and expeditiously. His name is Don Jarman, and he now lives in Wyoming.

I met Don in my hometown of Dublin, Georgia, in 1950. He was a brand new FBI agent, just out of training school at Quantico, Virginia, and his first assignment was the office in Savannah. Dublin was in his territory and he was in town once or twice a week.

Don was the first FBI agent I ever met. We hit it off right away. I was twenty-three and he was twenty-six. We were both single and ready for anything. It was because of my relationship with Don that I joined the FBI in 1954. He really loved rural Georgia, and having been raised in Wyoming on a ranch, he found many similarities. He knew that his stay in the Savannah office would be short, and he would be moving on to who knows where. But he was determined to enjoy every day of his Georgia stay.

Don was always happy and carefree, not a trouble in the world, and he was a hard worker to boot. But one day he came into Dublin with a long face, disappointment in his eyes. We had lunch together and that's when he broke the new to me.

"Been transferred," he said, getting right to the heart of the matter.

"Where?" I asked.

"New York," came the stoic reply.

The silence was deafening. After what seemed like an hour, I tried to break the quiet.

"Aw, you can handle it okay up there, Don. Heck, you might even learn to like it. You can tackle anything."

"Yeah, like you'd love to move to Russia."

"When do you have to be there?"

"Thirty days from yesterday."

"Great! I mean, at least we'll have time for a farewell shindig. We'll cook up some steaks, break open a bottle or two, and let the good times roll."

"I'd really appreciate that, Bo. Everybody here in Dublin has been mighty good to me. The police, the sheriff's office, the state patrol, everybody. I sure hate to think about leaving."

Two weeks later we all got together and gave Don one heck of a farewell party, including the deed to an acre of land near Dublin so he could come back whenever he wanted. That was on a Friday might. He left the next morning to drive the 986 miles to New York City.

Soon after he left, I received the following telegram from New York:

"Wouldn't live here if they gave me the whole damn island of Manhattan. Stop. Headed for Wyoming in the morning. Stop. Thanks for everything. Stop. Don."

So you see, it's not only the weak who can't cut it in the Big Apple. Don Jarman was strong—headstrong, that is.

The Butt of Many Jokes

I DON'T KNOW THAT A POLL HAS EVER BEEN taken regarding which city has been the butt of more jokes than any other, but if one is ever taken my money will be on New York. If for no other reason, New York has produced more comedians than all the other cities combined, and they don't hesitate to tell jokes on themselves.

As a longtime joke collector, I've pulled out my favorite Big Apple yuks.

A Westerner had recently moved to New York. Walking on a side street late one night, he was mugged.

"Give me your money or I'll blow your brains out," said the robber, brandishing a big gun.

"Blow away," said the man. "I don't need brains to live here."

A New York businessman visiting in Salt Lake City strolled about the city and made the acquaintance of a young Mormon lady.

"I'm from New York," he said. "Have you heard of it?"

"Oh, yes, sir!"

"You have?'

"Yes. Our church has a missionary there."

First southerner: "Were you in New York long enough to feel at home?"

Second southerner: "Sure. Why, I got so I could keep my seat in the subway car with a lady standing up and never even think twice about it."

The lonely stranger entered a restaurant in New York.

"May I take your order?" asked the waitress.

"Yes," said the customer. "I'd like two eggs, over easy, and a kind word."

The waitress brought the eggs and was moving away from the woman's table when the customer stopped her. "What about the kind word?" she asked.

"Don't eat the eggs," whispered the waitress.

Wife: "That new housekeeper of ours must be from New York. She calls the nursery the 'noisery.'"

Husband: "Well, I rather think that's the way it should be pronounced."

When the teacher asked her fifth grade class where the most ignorant people in the world could be found, a small boy held up his hand and quickly volunteered the answer.

"Yes, Robert."

"New York," he said.

Somewhat taken aback, the teacher asked him, "Where did you get your information?"

"Well, our geography book says that's where the population is the most dense."

A Cleveland man stopped a newsboy in New York and said to him, "See here, young man. I want to go to the Fifth National Bank. I'll give you a dollar if you direct me to it."

With a grin, the boy replied, "Okay. Follow me." He then led the man to a large building about one block away.

The man paid the promised fee, remarking, "Well, son, that was a dollar easily earned."

"Sure was," said the lad. "But you mustn't forget that bank directors are paid well in New York."

A visitor to the city stopped a New Yorker on the street and asked, "Excuse me, but do you have the correct time?"

"Sure do," said the man, as he walked away without missing a beat.

LIFE AIN'T FAIR

IT MAKES NO DIFFERENCE WHETHER AN OF-
fice has five employees or five hundred, there always seems to be one who is a little different, one
who stands out among the crowd. I worked in an office in New York with more than a thousand other
FBI agents, along with a warehouse full of stenogra-
phers, typists, and clerks. That was some thirty-five
years ago, and although I remember many of them
only vaguely, I remember one well—Jim Trainor,
from Pittsburgh.

Jim and I arrived in the New York office within a
few days of one another. We were the same age, and

we were assigned to the same squad, Bank Robbery and Fugitive.

Everybody has at one time or another seen a Jim Trainor. A former marine captain, the guy was Mr. Spit and Polish. He dressed as sharp as a tack, always neat and well groomed. Well, he was as well groomed as he could be with what he had to work with. His hair was disappearing fast, and it almost worried the guy to death. You might say it was an obsession.

At age thirty-four, Jim felt that it was his birthright to have a full crop of hair. But it was not meant to be. We all figured he'd be as bald as an egg before he turned thirty-six, and we ribbed him about it every chance we got.

Jim sat across from me in our squad room. We faced each other for the better part of four years. We worked together, ate together, bowled together, and we chased fugitives together. I saw him more than his wife did.

From the time Jim arrived at the office in the morning until he went home at night, he did one thing repeatedly. He would massage his scalp through his thinning, dark brown hair. He did it when viewing a file. He did it while dictating a report. He did it between turns at the bowling alley. He did it walking to the subway station.

I'll admit we were unkind to him. There were thirty-four of us on the squad, and not many days passed that one of us didn't say to Jim that his hair appeared to be getting thinner in one particular spot or another. That would only make him concentrate on that spot for the rest of the day.

He applied any number of so-called miracle potions to his scalp that were supposed to grow hair. I think he would have tried motor oil if someone had suggested it. And I know for a fact that he tried, among other things, overripe bananas, warm chocolate syrup, hot castor oil, Vaseline, and even Preparation H. No comment on that one.

One summer afternoon several of us were walking to lunch on Eighth Avenue, near Times Square. We passed two winos sitting on the sidewalk, leaning against a building. They were dirty, and drunk. Their hair was down in their faces, their pants were wet, and one had dried blood on an ear. After we had gone about four or five steps passed the two, Jim stopped dead in his tracks.

"Look at 'em!" he said. "I'll bet neither one of 'em has shampooed his hair since World War II, and both have full heads of hair! It's not fair. And I'll bet neither one has owned a toothbrush in years. But I'll guarantee you that neither of 'em has a single cavity. Personal hygiene? Forget it. They don't know the meaning of the term. Yet they are probably healthy as two horses. Give 'em a bath and both would lose ten pounds in dirt alone. I'm telling you, it's just not fair. What do you bet they both live to be a hundred?"

I haven't seen or heard from Jim in years, but I sure hope his hair grew back. Thinking of Jim makes me wonder how those two drunks are doing. They're probably still on Eighth Avenue, still drunk, still sporting full heads of hair.

Redneck Women?
You Betcha'!

I'VE TRAVELED THIS COUNTRY FROM ONE end to the other for the past eleven years peddling books and answering questions about rednecks. The second most asked questions of me is "Are there redneck women?" You bet your white boots and ragged jeans there are. The most asked question? "What is a redneck?"

For the benefit of my New York friends, most of whom have never seen a redneck woman or pulled up to the counter in a south Georgia juke joint, permit me to educate you on the subject. The redneck woman has been ignored for too long. I am an equal opportunity writer, and the women deserve recognition as well as the men. So here goes.

A redneck woman:

- Suggests to her date that his sideburns are too long.

- Has red marks below the knees from wearing boots.

- Grew up wanting to be Dolly Parton but ended up waiting tables at the Waffle House.

- Never discos. Instead, she prefers line dancing.

- Uses either Foxy Lady or Country Sunshine as her CB handle.

- Is usually named Ruby, Betty, Gladys, or Mabel.

- Is never named Kelli, Penelope, Heather, or Sheri.

- Doesn't mind sitting at the bar alone.

- Will go out to dinner as long as it's fried.

- Thinks racquetball is a fancy new pinball machine.

- Doesn't own a tennis outfit.

- Can lift a watermelon by herself.

- Always sits in the middle on a date.

- Never drinks white wine.

- Never needs a glass for her beer.

- Is loyal to the end.

- Doesn't mind Vitalis hair.

- Has pictures of her old boyfriends in her wallet, and one of Elvis.

- Can bait her own hook.

- Doesn't cry—she gets even.

- Thinks stock-car racing is the great American pastime.

- Sets all her car radio buttons to country stations.

- Keeps her beer and jukebox money in her shirt pocket.

- Likes plastic shoes better than leather.

- Shops at K-Mart in curlers.

- Asks you to dance.

- Cleans the fish without complaining.

- Has no desire to get into real estate or public relations.

- Not only doesn't mind wearing a helmet, but will also change the motorcycle's oil.

- Would rather ride in a motorboat than go sailing.

- Can roll a cigarette.

- Cooks everything well done.

- Would rather go to the Grand Ole Opry than the Academy Awards.

- Doesn't know—or care—where the Mason-Dixon line is.

- Has never seen *Gone with the Wind*.

- Can feed her baby while playing the guitar.

- Thinks living in a double-wide is the living end.

- Wants to be Redneck Woman of the Year and win a free trip to Opryland.

- Smokes Salem Light 100's and drinks longneck Buds.

- Holds allegiance to her "mommer en diddy."

- Spends Sundays down to the river.

STRANGER IN A STRANGE LAND

IT'S ONE THING TO BE UNABLE TO UNDER-stand New Yorkese, but even worse is not being able to understand or speak one word of English while living in the midst of those who can. Here is a story that I feel illustrates the predicament of just such a man.

He was well into his eighties and had never left his native country until he came to live with his son in New York. For weeks after his arrival he never left his son's apartment. His son would go to work and the old man would sit in his room, brooding for the old country and the friends he'd left there to come to America.

His son, sensing his father's unhappiness, suggested that he get out of the apartment while he was at work and walk around. He went further and suggested that he visit the small restaurant located several blocks from his apartment and maybe get a bite to eat and something to drink. Surprisingly, the old gentleman agreed and said he would go the following morning. But he also pointed out one problem, that because he spoke no English he would not be able to order anything to eat.

The son sat his father down in his small kitchen and taught him to say "apple pie and coffee." He practiced all night, over and over, repeating "appla pie anda coffee," "appla pie anda coffee," "appla pie anda coffee," until he had it down to perfection. He could hardly wait for morning to arrive.

No sooner had his son left for work than the old man walked to the little restaurant, some ten blocks away. It was practically empty and the waitress approached him almost immediately.

"Morning. What'll ya' have?" she asked.

"Appla pie anda coffee," he replied with some understandable degree of apprehension.

She returned soon with his order and he thoroughly enjoyed his apple pie and coffee. His routine of boredom and brooding had been broken.

Every morning for several weeks the old gentleman made the morning trek to the little restaurant and ordered "appla pie anda coffee." He and the waitress became quite friendly, although he spoke no other English.

Finally, one night, the old gentleman said to his son, in his native language, as he drew his forefinger across his neck, "I'm uppa to here with appla pie anda coffee. Teach me how to say something else."

The son understood his father's wish and suggested that he learn to say "ham and eggs." His father smiled and began practicing for the next morning, pleased that he would get something different to eat as well as surprise his new friend, the waitress.

He practiced his new saying well into the night, and on his way to the little restaurant the next morning he repeated "hama anda eggs" as he walked.

At the restaurant he took his usual seat and the waitress greeted him and started to walk to the kitchen. He motioned with his hand for her to come to his table.

"Apple pie and coffee?" she asked.

He shook his head negatively, smiled, and said, "Hama anda eggs."

"Okay. Do you want your eggs scrambled, over well, medium, sunny side up, well done, or poached?" she asked with order pad in hand and pen at the ready.

A look of disappointment came over the old man's face. He lowered his head slightly and mumbled softly with a note of resignation and defeat in his voice, "Appla pie anda coffee."

DOWN SOUTH EATIN' UP NORTH

If you're visiting the Big Apple and find yourself overcome with cravings for real food—fried, mashed, or covered with gravy—here are a few restaurants to try when you've got a hankering for home:

- Cafe Beulah: 39 East 19th St., 212-777-9700
- Emily's Restaurant: 1325 5th Ave. (11th St.), 212-996-1212
- Jezebel: 630 9th Ave. at 45th St., 212-582-1045
- Snooky's Cafe: 63 West 137th St. (between Lenox & 5th Aves.), 212-281-3500
- Sylvia's: 328 Lenox Ave. at 126th St., 212-996-0660
- Tennessee Mountain: 143 Spring St., 212-431-3993

FOOD FIGHTS

I HAD ALWAYS PROMISED MYSELF THAT IF I ever got to New York City in the wintertime I would make a point to visit Rockefeller Center and watch the ice skaters glide around the skating rink like I had seen them do on television. I got my chance in January 1990.

I flew to the Big Apple from Atlanta to attend a surprise party for my best friend, Winston Groom, given by his wife, Rosemarie, on the occasion of his seventieth birthday. They lived in New Jersey, in a town about an hour by bus from New York City. I stayed with them for three days and took advantage

81

of the opportunity to fulfill the promise to myself to visit Rockefeller Center and watch the skaters.

It was near lunchtime when I arrived, so I took a table by the window in the restaurant overlooking the rink and made a big New York mistake—I ordered lunch.

The sandwich was delicious, the hot coffee soothing, and the view of the skaters great. I was glad I had come, and I stayed for more than an hour. When I asked the waitress for my check, I felt like somebody had pulled the plug on my life support system—$17.85, plus eight percent sales tax and a fifteen percent gratuity. The grand total was $20.60!

I had never in my life paid $1.50 for a cup of coffee, or $15.25 for a turkey sandwich. I just sat there, dumbfounded. Then I thought about my father-in-law and great friend, Joe Sapp, and his one and only trip to New York.

Mr. Joe, as everybody called him, loved baseball almost as much as he did his daughter. He and his good friend, Gordon Tucker, decided to attend the 1962 World Series between the New York Yankees and the San Francisco Giants. When they returned to their little hometown of Pulaski, Georgia, Gordon told two stories on Mr. Joe. Mr. Joe always laughed the loudest.

As Gordon loved to tell it, Mr. Joe wanted to find a nice restaurant and get a real good steak. Everybody back home knew what a steak fancier he was. So they struck out from their hotel to locate the proper place.

After walking around Manhattan for quite a while, they came upon what appeared to be a very nice restaurant, the Beef Barn, and walked inside. After a long wait, the maitre d' seated them. Shortly thereafter, a waiter appeared.

"Good evening, gentlemen. My name is Ricky and I'll be your waiter this evening."

"Nice to meet cha', Ricky," said Gordon, offering his hand. "I'm Gordon and this here's Joe."

"Yes . . . uh . . . well . . . Would you like a drink?"

Mr. Joe, always the conservative one, said, "Yes. I'd like a glass of ice water."

"Me too," said Gordon, following suit.

Ricky frowned and disappeared, but he returned quickly, holding a tray with two glasses of ice water.

"Now then, would you like to hear about our specials this evening?" Ricky chirped.

Mr. Joe and Gordon nodded. Ricky began his spiel, rattling off the specials in a monotone. "We have a delicious 12-ounce sirloin covered with a mushroom sauce for $28.95, a wonderful 10-ounce Delmonico priced at $25.75, a great 14-ounce T-bone for $24.95, and the chef's choice tonight, a 16-ounce porterhouse for just $34.50."

Mr. Joe said nothing, but stared intently at Ricky's chin to the point where Ricky seemed somewhat nervous.

"Then, we have the specialty of the house, a 12-ounce filet served with baked potato, green beans, and a garden salad for just $35.00," Ricky said, concluding his presentation.

Mr. Joe continued to stare at Ricky's chin. Finally, Ricky asked him, "Is there something wrong with my chin? You seem quite fascinated by it."

"No, there's nothing wrong with your chin," said

Mr. Joe. "It's just that I've never seen a chin with a hole in it like yours has."

"Oh, why that's my dimple," explained Ricky, somewhat proudly.

"I see," said Mr. Joe.

"Do you have a problem with that?"

"No," responded Mr. Joe. "It's just that everything is so high here I thought it might be your navel!"

The night before they returned to Georgia from New York, Gordon and Mr. Joe decided to go all out and treat themselves to a real nice dinner in a five-star restaurant. They chose one in the theater district that celebrities were rumored to frequent on a regular basis. The pair's grocery bills for a week wouldn't have equaled the tab. But they didn't care. They were on vacation, living it up, letting it all hang out.

They both agreed that the dinner was superb and the service excellent. Their waiter, Pierre, had left no stone unturned to ensure that their evening was a success. He even persuaded Jackie Gleason and Mary Martin to autograph menus for them, and Mickey Mantle posed with them at their table for a photograph.

"How was your dinner, gentlemen?" asked Pierre.

"Great!" said Gordon.

"Real good," said the ever conservative Mr. Joe.

"That's good," said Pierre. "I'm glad. Would you care for dessert?"

"No, thank you," said Gordon. "I couldn't eat another bite."

"And how about you, sir?" Pierre inquired of Mr. Joe.

"Does it come with the meal?"

"Oh, yes, sir. Also an after dinner drink if you'd like one."

"Okay. I'll take a piece of pie and a glass of water."

"Very good, sir. And what kind of pie would you like?"

"What? What do you mean what kind of pie?" shouted Mr. Joe. "Sweet potato pie, of course. What the hell do you think pies are made out of?"

DINING OUT WITH OLD GATOR MINCEY

WHEN YOU LIVE AND WORK IN PLACES LIKE Las Vegas, Orlando, Los Angeles, Denver, Vail, Aspen, or New York, you get calls from people you never heard of claiming to be long-lost cousins or former classmates. "Just visiting for a few days and thought I'd give you a call," they say. What they're really doing is looking for a free place to sleep or free tickets to certain events peculiar to your location.

When I was living and working in New York, I received a call late one night from a fella who I had gone to high school with, Gator Mincey.

"Just called to say howdy," he said.

"Good to hear from you, Gator. Where are you?"

"Over heah at th' Duncan Truck Stop in Jersey City. Brought a load o' watermelons up heah f'r old man Roberts. 'Member him?"

"Sure," I said. "I must have stolen a hundred watermelons from him over the years!"

"Me too!"

"How long are you gonna be in town?" I asked.

"Jus' 'til in a' mornin'. I'll unload an' head on back," Gator allowed.

"I'd sure like to see you. How 'bout if I come get you and you spend the night with me and we can talk over old times?"

"I'd rilly lak to but if'n I did they wouldn' be a watermelon lef' on this truck when I got back. More thieves ovah heah than y' can shake a stick at."

"Well, how 'bout tomorrow night? You can park your truck at my place and we'll go out to eat. Do you really have to leave tomorrow?"

"Well, uh, naw, now that y' mention it. This is th' last load o' th' season. So I s'pose I could stay ovah, if'n I wouldn' be no bother to ya."

"Good. I'll come over in the morning and you can follow me back here. Okay?"

"Fine. Ya' know how to' git heah?"

"Oh, yeah. I'm very familiar with Duncan's."

"Okay. See ya' in t' mornin' then."

"Good."

I looked forward to seeing Gator again. I remembered him well from our high school days together, although he had been two years ahead of me. Gator was far and away the toughest boy in school. Heck, he was the toughest boy in the entire county. Nobody, but nobody, challenged that. But while Gator was tough, he wasn't mean. Everybody liked him.

As a boy he lived with his daddy in a shack on the edge of the Okefenokee Swamp, near the Florida line. Mr. Mincey owned an alligator farm on U.S. Highway 1, and during the tourist season, in summer, Gator wrestled the alligators every afternoon to the delight of the tourists.

I remember that when Gator was in the tenth grade, he went out for the football team. But the coach had to cut him from the squad because the first week of practice Gator banged up so many of his teammates that there weren't enough left for a scrimmage. So, he turned to wrestling and won the Georgia State Championship the next three years.

Gator had numerous scholarship offers after graduation to play college football and wrestle, but he turned them down. "I jus' want to stay heah with my daddy," he would say. So he did.

We went to a fine New York restaurant and Gator was in awe. It was a far cry from Hamby's Cafe in Waycross, Georgia. And I can tell you that the night was quite an experience for me as well. The menu was the size of two pieces of plywood, and Gator was completely baffled by it.

"Are you ready to order, sir?" asked our waiter.

"Tell ya' what, hoss. Jus' bring me page two with a little buttah an' hot sauce," said Gator.

The waiter failed to see the humor in that, so I suggested the prime rib.

"It's delicious, Gator," I said.

"All right, I'll try it. How big is it?"

"It's twelve ounces," said the waiter.

"Okay. Bring me two of 'em, with a bunch o' French fries an' a glass o' ice tea. Sweet."

"Did you say two of them, sir?"

"Yep, two."

"Very good, sir. And how would you like them prepared?"

"Well done."

"Well done, sir?"

"Whassa' matter, ain't I talkin' loud 'nuff for ya'? I said well done. Jus' go ahead an' cremate 'em."

"Very good, sir."

I ordered the same, only one, medium rare.

The meat looked great when our waiter brought our orders. But it wasn't long before I saw Gator motion with his finger for the waiter to come back to the table.

"Yes?"

"I wanted these two pieces o' meat cooked well done. I seen cows down home get hurt worse 'en this and git up and run off. Take 'em back and tell the cook t' burn the suckers," demanded Gator.

It was done, and when they were returned, black as soot, Gator seemed happy. He tucked his napkin into his collar and said, "That's bettah. Where's the catch-up?"

"For the prime rib, sir?" asked the waiter.

"Right."

"Oh my! Excuse me. I'll be right back."

Gator got his "catch-up," even though the request seemed to break the waiter's heart.

The food was great, and Gator cleaned his plate.

When the waiter returned with the finger bowls, before I could say anything to Gator, he had loaded his up with salt and pepper and slurped it right down.

"Great food," he said through a muted burp.

Gator lit a cigarette and leaned back to relax. The maitre d' stopped at our table and asked, "Was your dinner to your satisfaction, gentlemen?"

"Oh, yeah!" exclaimed Gator. "But that bowl o' soup was a li'l weak."

I said nothing, just paid the check and left. Gator is just Gator, and always will be. Nothing more, nothing less.

No Breakfast at Tiffany's

I HAD BEEN LIVING AND WORKING IN THE New York area for almost a year in June 1964. I hadn't learned as much as I wanted to, but I had learned something about the temperaments of New Yorkers.

I had been told by some people—supposedly in the know—that New Yorkers, as a group, have no sense of humor. How could that be, I wondered. Hadn't they given us countless comedians? *All in the Family?* Anyway, I decided to try and find out for myself one sunny day that summer.

I decided to bum around the city all day long, with nothing planned or organized. As I gazed out of the bus window as it droned toward the Lincoln

Tunnel and the Port Authority Bus Terminal (known back home as the bus station), I thought how lucky I was to have a day off in such a great city as New York. I stepped off the bus and hadn't walked very far before I saw a huge sign: "June Special—*Breakfast at Tiffany's* with Audrey Hepburn and George Peppard—Only $4.50 All Month."

Having been a little mischievous all my life, at age forty I hadn't changed much. Eating breakfast with Audrey and George seemed like a good idea, and for a mere $4.50 a real bargain in New York. Plus, it was 9:30 A.M. and I hadn't eaten yet. This would be a good time to test the humor level of New Yorkers, I thought to myself. No sense of humor? I'd find out for myself. I window-shopped my way along Fifth Avenue, enjoying the expensive scenery, until I spotted Tiffany's. I knew I would have a fun time in there. I wasn't exactly dressed properly for a visit to this Fort Knox of the jewelry world, wearing a plaid sport shirt, khakis, a western belt, no socks, and loafers. If I'd had ten or twenty thousand bucks in my pockets the folks at Tiffany's would have no doubt characterized me as an eccentric. I didn't, and they didn't. Instead, I had close to thirty dollars on me, and it didn't take them long to write me off as a hayseed.

I checked my trusty Timex—10:25 A.M.—and walked in like I was loaded. A young lady greeted me, although somewhat reluctantly.

"May I be of some help to you?" she asked.

"Uh, yes ma'am," I replied in my best Rhett Butler accent. "Have Audrey and George done got heah yet?"

"Who?"

"Audrey Hepburn and George Peppard. The sign said they'd be heah all this month to have breakfast with y'r customers an' I jus' come by to eat with 'em and say howdy. I sure likes both of 'em."

"Sign? What sign?"

"Th' one up at th' bus station. I think y'all got a real good promotion goin' heah."

"Promotion? Tell me, just what did the sign say, exactly, sir?"

"Well, lemme' see . . . best I can recall it said 'June Special—*Breakfast at Tiffany's* with Audrey Hepburn and George Peppard—Only $4.50 All Month.' That sounded lak a real good deal t' me, so heah I am."

"I see. Well, let me assure you that neither Audrey Hepburn or George Peppard will be here for breakfast. Not today. Not tomorrow. Not all month. The sign you saw obviously refers to the movie *Breakfast at Tiffany's,* starring Audrey Hepburn and George Peppard, and some movie theater must be running a special this month for $4.50 per ticket."

"Well, I'll just be dadblamed. I never thought of it that way."

"Obviously."

"I thank ya', ma'am. But you sure y'all don't serve breakfast heah?"

"No! We never have and we never will. Good day, sir!"

I walked to the door and heard the lady speak to one of her co-workers.

"Tell me, Anna, why do I get the hayseeds?"

"You're just lucky, I guess," came the response.

I concluded that at least one female New Yorker really doesn't have a sense of humor, especially when she's dealing with a hayseed like me. Still, I would have loved to have eaten breakfast with Audrey and George.

GETTING AROUND TOWN

THE FIRST-TIME VISITOR TO NEW YORK CITY will more than likely rely on taxicabs to get around the city. That depends, of course, on his or her economic status. It's possible to go through an inheritance using taxis in New York. I recall that during my first visit, of a three-day duration during Thanksgiving 1954, I went through a house payment, a car payment, and a paycheck on taxis alone. Most who commute from neighboring states are apt to scoot around the city in automobiles playing "dodge cars" on their appointed rounds. This can be dangerous, and expensive. One look at New York traffic and it's not hard to understand why insurance rates are so high. Sherman tanks and bulldozers could make out all right, but automobiles are doomed from the time their motors are started. Drivers don't even bother to stop when they hit another car. Just "slam bam, thank you ma'am," and they continue on their way.

And pity the poor pedestrian. Walking across the street for him is like tiptoeing through a mine field. He knows he's going to get hit, but just doesn't know when. And whether the light is red or green is of no consequence.

There was a story making the rounds when I worked in New York in the 1960s about an elderly gentleman who waited patiently at a traffic light for the WALK signal. When it came, he started across the street only to be hit by a car driven by an elderly woman who had run a red light. She hit her brakes and skidded some forty-five feet after hitting him, rolled down her window, and yelled back to him, "Watch out!"

The man panicked, threw up his hands, and yelled in response, "Oh, no! What are you gonna' do, lady? Back up?"

Then, there was the country boy from Alabama who was visiting the Big Apple on a high school trip. One night he slipped out of his hotel room only to wander the streets of Manhattan and get lost. He called the hotel and spoke to one of the class chaperones.

"All right, tell me where you are and I'll hail a cab and come get you," said the chaperone.

"I don't know where I am. I just know I'm in the middle of a bunch of tall buildings," he said.

"Well, just look at the signs at the intersection and tell me where you are."

"All right, just a minute I'll be right back."

After a lengthy pause, the chaperone heard the boy say, "I'm at the corner of WALK and DON'T WALK."

Native New Yorkers don't hesitate, they ride the subways. Visitors shy away from them like the plague. The media have convinced them that on their first ride they will either be robbed, shot, or raped—or possibly all three. And it's a known fact that New Yorkers can't drive. No prejudice, it's just a fact. Oh, they try. But how can they ever learn to drive by moving twelve feet and stopping? They put on their brakes a lot, curse even more, all the while honking their horns. None of these is an established driving aid. They continue to drive twelve more feet, stop, wait, and then drive twelve more feet.

A gigantic problem in New York is parking. A New Yorker would much rather have a reserved parking space than have his pension benefits tripled. Contrary to what you see on television and in the movies, there's never any place to park in the city. There always a parking place in the movies or on television for the stars, right in the busiest section of Manhattan. That's a fantasy world. Try finding a parking spot in real life and see what happens. Either your car gets towed, you get a parking ticket, or you get in a fight. If you're planning a trip to New York, here are a few tips for riding the subway, which will save you a lot of money over taxis. You'll need it to pay for dinner.

If the person standing next to you suddenly decides to commit murder or strangle his girlfriend, don't interfere. Keep reading your newspaper until you reach the next stop. Then get off.

No matter how crowded a car looks, there's always room for one more. Don't let anybody tell you otherwise. Just lower your shoulders and go for it.

Play it safe with pickpockets and thieves. Use an Ace bandage and secure your wallet in your armpit before boarding.

Do not yell "Here's a vacant seat!" in an attempt to be neighborly. That's worse than yelling "Fire" in the theater.

If a group of young men wearing black leather jackets and earrings, with skeletons and crossbones on their foreheads, suddenly appears and asks for your wallet, give it to them. This is not the time to be a hero.

Never volunteer to help an old lady with her paper bags filled with who knows what. Do it, and she'll hit you over the head with her cane and run, shouting to the high heavens and to every policeman in New York that you're a thief—or worse.

Once on board, push and shove to your heart's content. That's the name of the subway game.

Make every effort not to be the first one to enter or the last one to exit. You could be crushed or trampled to death, and no one would ever notice.

Never offer a woman your seat. If you do, you will hear profanity you never knew existed, no matter if you were in the navy.

Finally, never ask directions in a subway situation, not even from a policeman. A cattle rancher from Wyoming, on his first visit to New York, did so after coming out of Grand Central Station into the confusion of Forty-second Street.

He walked over to a traffic officer, who was very busy, and said, "Mister, I want to go to Central Park."

"Okay, Sonny," said the officer. "You can go this time, but don't ask me again."

BOWERY BOYS

THE BOWERY IS A STREET IN NEW YORK CITY, but more commonly known is the district surrounding it that is characterized by flophouses, saloons, and alcoholics. Men with no hope left inhabit the district and wait to die. More than three hundred people die each day in the Big Apple, many of them on the streets and in the flophouses of the Bowery.

It is perhaps the only spot in New York where the standard of living never goes up. Sick, sad, and shameful, the Bowery residents are a cross section of America with men who once headed corporations, enjoyed prestigious and profitable law practices, performed on elite stages and in first run movies, until the bottle grabbed and choked them. Now they try to live through the day, to hell with tomorrow. A drink, any drink, begins their day.

The men of the Bowery appear on the streets unshaven, unclean, and unwashed. They know not where their next bite of food will come from. To watch them live is a pitiful sight. To watch them die is almost a relief, realizing that their cares and worries are over, at least on this earth. And when they die they die as they lived—alone. All their worldly goods consist of the clothes they have on and what is in their pockets. They are the unknown, the neglected, and the uncared for in New York, a blotch on the face of a great city. The Bowery Boys are an entity unto themselves. Every time I went to the Bowery and saw the depth to which humanity can fall, I was reminded of a plaque that hangs on the wall behind the bar in a Bowery saloon. The inscription, which read something like this, was probably written by one who had taken the big fall:

"I've known the love of a beautiful woman,
And the love of a wonderful mother.
But never in my life have I ever seen,
Such love as one drunken bum has for another."

You watch them and wonder, "How in the world can six-year-old whiskey whip a fifty-year-old man?" But it does. It plays no favorites, and position and prominence make no difference.

On any given day, or night, one sound dominates the sidewalks of the Bowery: "Say, mistah, got a quarter?"

Who is he? How did he land, face down, in the Bowery? There's a Lockheed engineer who drank himself out of a job; a television actor who once starred on a top rated show; a Harvard professor who spent four jobless years on the Bowery before stumbling into a mission for help; a preacher who failed to heed his own advice delivered in his sermons; a concert pianist whose talented fingers once played the classics to the delight of thousands in concert halls both in America and Europe, but now hold a bottle, shakily; a star major league baseball player, a great hitter who struck out when the bottle made its pitch.

Some Bowery men may seek help, but many more hit the low level and remain there, with nowhere else to go. Some stay on the Bowery by choice.

One who sticks out in my memory was "Bozo," Frederick Aloysius Clark, who was born in Provincetown, Massachusetts, around 1892.

Bozo claims to have gone to sea as a teenager, and later spent several years touring with carnivals, first as a handyman, later as a target for a ball-throwing concession, and finally as a ballyhoo artist for a troupe of hoochy-coochee dancers called the "Eight Virgin Rosebuds."

He admits to three marriages, all brief and unpleasant, and says with a gleam in his eye that common-law marriages are the best. When asked if he has any children, his standard reply is always, "Well, let me put it like this. Every time I walk past an orphanage I throw some pennies over the wall—I want my kids to get some."

With his freeloading and the small pension he says he gets from participating in the Mexican border dispute in 1914, Bozo says he manages to live about as well as he wishes.

According to him, New York is a good city for bums, but adds quickly that he wouldn't want to die in New York and be buried with the city's unclaimed dead and paupers in Potter's Field.

Sometimes Bozo becomes so lonely and morose on the Bowery that he switches from beer and wine to hard liquor, goes on a drunken tear and nobody sees him for weeks. Later he is usually found in the gutter with his face dirty, bruised and bloody, for when he goes on a binge he is obnoxious, insults bigger Bowery men, and they slug him down. But he sobers up, and a few days later he's again the happy, beer drinking intellectual in Sammy's Saloon who backslaps, and laughs, and poses for pictures with the tourists, and says, "Five years ago I was a bum. Now look at me. I'm no ordinary bum. I'm a classical, dynamic, intellectual panhandler."

Bozo is a fixture on the Bowery, and probably couldn't survive any place else. With his drinking buddies dying all around him, he still laughs.

A DIFFERENT KIND
OF NEIGHBORHOOD

ALONG WITH SOFT PRETZELS, LONG COM-
mutes, and great theater, I was introduced to the
concept of ethnic neighborhoods when I moved to
the Big Apple. This was as foreign to me as were the
Russian, Chinese, and Swahili languages I often
heard spoken on the subway.

The first priority upon being transferred from one
FBI office to another is to locate suitable housing for
the family. This I had done previously when transferred from Washington, DC, to Houston, Texas;
from Houston to Corpus Christi; from Corpus
Christi to Beaumont; from Beaumont to Detroit,
Michigan; from Detroit to Marquette. Now, I was

house hunting again, in the New York-New Jersey area. Not a pleasant task, but one that had to be done.

After several days, many maps, and an armload of brochures from real estate and rental offices, I found what appeared to be a possibility in a small town in New Jersey. It was an older house that had been remodeled. It was just a few blocks from the train station, and the area schools had a good reputation. Commuting time to New York, a prime consideration, was forty-five minutes by train. The church was nearby and a nice little shopping center was but four blocks away.

During my search for suitable housing, I heard repeated references to "ethnic neighborhoods." The term was foreign to me. In the small towns where I grew up in south Georgia, everybody sort of lived in one bunch. People mixed and mingled around the courthouse square, at basketball games, in front of grocery stores, in the barber shop, at peanut boilings, at cane grindings, and at hog and cow sales. What nationality were most of these people? Southern. But if they hadn't been, I don't think the rest of us would have cared.

After renting the neat, three-bedroom house with a nice yard, I called my family back in Georgia. Then, back at the office, I spread the word to my fellow agents. I described the house in detail, including the street on which it was located.

"Oh, yeah," said one. "I had a friend who lived over there a few years ago. It's an Italian neighborhood."

"An Italian neighborhood?" I asked.

"Right."

"Anything wrong with that?"

"No, not a thing. I just mentioned it for your information."

"We didn't have neighborhoods where I grew up. Not enough people to divide up. The closest things to them, I guess, were sections. The rich folks lived in their section on one side of the railroad tracks and the common folks had their section on the other side."

So, we moved in—me, my wife, and our son and daughter. The house was comfortable but not pretentious. And we were truly in an Italian neighborhood.

To our right was Anthony Collucci and his family, with six children. To our left was Charley Siatta and his family, including five children and a mother-in-law. Directly across the street was Joseph Colombo and his family, with four children and a mother-in-law. All of these people took us in and showed us— among other things—the joy of eating Italian food.

Every weekend was a picnic. We cooked outside in summer and inside in winter. I've never been a big man—six foot one and 175 pounds. That's what I weighed when I moved in. I was still six foot one when I moved out four years later, but I weighed in at 194.

Mary Collucci, Tony's wife, made by far the best chicken cacciatore on this earth. It was sinful to eat it the way I did, and with almost a loaf of her delicious garlic bread at every sitting. Charley Siatta allowed no one in his household to prepare spaghetti but himself, and he guarded his recipe for meat sauce with more secrecy than the Coca-Cola formula. He was known all over town as the best spaghetti maker around. Joe Columbo's wife, Anna, would put Italian chefs in leading New York restaurants to shame with her ravioli. Ravioli was more than a dish to her—it was a creation of blue ribbon quality.

My contribution to the food fest? Barbecued ribs and homemade peach ice cream, made in a hand-churned freezer. I was good at it. None better.

Those were good days. Before I left to return to Georgia I was proud of the fact that Mary Colluci had been converted. She was eating boiled peanuts, and loving them. She never got turned on to grits, however. But I tried.

No way will I ever forget my great friends. They always made me and my family feel welcome in their homes. A fellow just doesn't forget things like that, especially when he's on foreign soil a thousand miles away from his roots.

LIFE ON THE STREETS

THIS IS NOT A STORY FOR THE BRIDGE CLUB, but it's real. That's the only reason I included it in this book. It's real and it's about a real person. All New Yorkers don't live on Park Avenue, but all New Yorkers live—somewhere. Some live on the streets, existing by the mere skin of their teeth.

Let me say early on that this is a story about a whore. If you can't take a story about a whore, then I'd advise against reading any further. Hers is a story of a disentegrated life. I knew her and her sad story well. Multiply it by the thousands and you'll know what life is like for people on the streets of New York.

The woman's name was Speedie. I knew her in the early 1960s when she was in her twenties. She was beautiful: dark olive skin, flawless complexion, jet black hair, dark eyes, medium height, and a bathing suit figure. She was a rookie in the sex business. That was obvious when she offered to sell herself to me, an FBI agent, as I walked along Eighth Avenue. She panicked when I identified myself, showing my badge and credentials. I assured her that I wasn't going to arrest her. I couldn't, even if I'd been so inclined. Prostitution is not in itself a federal crime. Being transported across state lines for the purpose of prostitution is, but not for the woman. The person who transports her across is the one the feds are interested in. A pimp can get up to five years and a $10,000 fine. It's called the White Slave Traffic Act, or the Mann Act.

Speedie told me that she had been in New York but four days when she hit on me. "Just my luck," she laughed. "I'm here less than a week and I proposition a fed."

"Be careful," I said. "And here's my card if you ever want to see me again."

"On official business, I suppose?"

"You're absolutely right about that."

I guess in my twenty years in the FBI I probably talked to more whores than Heidi Fleiss. Speedie was sort of special because of the circumstances that put her on the streets in the first place, and because of the end that came to her. Her story has been in my craw for thirty years, now revealed here for the first time. It proves, if nothing else, I guess, that no one is exempt from the gutter.

The young woman had what should have been a beautiful career ahead of her at age twenty-two. She hailed from a midwestern state and a fine family. Two brothers and a sister. A mother who taught school and a father who was a successful druggist. Speedie was an A student in a fine university. In her junior year she won the right to represent her state in the Miss America Pageant. She didn't finish last, either. Much higher than that. Her talent was singing. Just hearing her talk was like listening to a lullaby.

Shortly after the pageant a man approached her and introduced himself as a talent scout for a well-known New York agent. "I cover the Midwest," he said. "You are very talented. I heard you sing in Atlantic City and told my boss about you. He would like for you to come to New York for some auditions. All expenses paid, of course. Will you consider it? If so, I'll get back in touch with you in a few weeks when I'm in town again."

Speedie was from a relatively small town, and she was easily impressed. She glowed at the possibility of a professional singing career. The man did contact her again. She accepted his offer to travel to New York for auditions. She made a terrible mistake. She went, but she never came back.

Speedie was met at LaGuardia Airport by the man who had first contacted her. He was driving a late model Cadillac. That impressed her. He wore beautiful jewelry. That impressed her. His suit and shirt were tailor made. That impressed her. He took her to a cheap hotel, with drop lights from the ceiling and exposed plumbing. That didn't impress her.

The truth came out quickly. Her escort was a pimp. She wanted to leave, but he wouldn't let her. From the moment she walked with him into that hotel room she was his prisoner. He ler her know right off that he expected her to sell her body and give him the money. Speedie was crushed. She had never before engaged in sexual intercourse.

He told her what to do and how to do it. He told her what areas to work on the streets and where to take the men to have sex. He watched her like a hawk, and he took all the proceeds.

On one occasion, about six months after her arrival in New York, she tried to get away from him and go to the police. He caught her, took her to his apartment in the Bronx, beat her with his fists, and slashed her back with a straight razor. It required forty-seven stitches to close the wound.

I must have talked with Speedie more than a hundred times, but never alone. That's an FBI no-no. She was easy to talk to, and she could have testified and sent her pimp, Pretty Boy, to prison. But she didn't. Like most, she was afraid. Who could blame her?

I left New York in 1964 and moved back to Georgia. I received a phone call one night about a year later from an agent in our New York office. He had a number for me to call, a detective in New York who wanted to talk with me. Our conversation was short.

"Do you know a street hustler here in New York named Speedie?"

"Yes," I answered.

"What can you tell me about her?"

"You know better than that. What can *you* tell me about her?"

"Well, for starters, she's dead. Apparent overdose."

"Why did you call me?"

"I found your card underneath her mattress. Was she an informant?"

"No. She was a source, and a good one for me when I worked in New York."

"Are you at liberty to tell me anything more?"

"Sure," I said, and I told him what she'd told me, including how she came to be in New York in the first place.

"Sounds like she was a nice lady before meeting Pretty Boy."

"Yes, she was. Came from a nice family, as far as I could tell."

"Well, you might like to know that Pretty Boy is now doing ten to twenty for pandering and numerous drug violations."

"Thanks. I'll sleep a little better now."

"Fine. And thanks for your help."

"You're more than welcome."

I remembered what Speedie told me once when I asked her why prostitutes needed pimps.

"Well, it's like this," she said. "It's always refreshing for a whore to wake up every morning, turn over, and look at her pimp and realize that there is someone in the world who is lower down than she is."

GREAT STUFF YOU WON'T FIND IN THE METROPOLITAN MUSEUM OF ART

- Elvis on velvet
- Bottle trees
- Chainsaw sculptures
- Dogs playing poker
- Tire planters
- Hubcap collections
- Plastic flamingos

BATTLE FATIGUE

YOU RUN INTO THEM WHEREVER YOU GO: Chicago, Atlanta, Miami, Detroit, Los Angeles, Seattle, Carbondale, Willacoochee, Dublin, Allentown, Shawnee, or New York City. They're known universally as smartasses. I seem to attract them like a watermelon attracts flies. Smartasses are worse. They're a lot like hemorrhoids—they're a pain in the butt and they won't go away.

Only one person can solve all the world's problems, has all the answers, and wherever you sit he's usually in the chair right next to you. I go to a football game at the University of Georgia to see the Bulldogs play and there he is, in the next seat. He's an authority, a fat, loud, self-proclaimed football expert who guzzles bourbon and smokes smelly cigars. He got a twenty-four-hour head start on the bourbon and has a shirt pocket full of cigars.

"The dawgs ain't gonna' do it today," he announces to one and all.

"Why not?" I ask, immediately wishing I hadn't.

"Simple. 'Cause Coach Dooley ain't been usin' his big yard dawg right, that's why," he says authoritatively.

"His big yard dawg?"

"Right. Herschel Walker. Dooley jus' ain't makin' th' best use of th' boy."

"How do you mean?"

"When th' game starts I'll show ya'."

Meanwhile he finishes off a fifth of bourbon, lights up an-other stale rope, and succeeds in insulting the sweet young thing three seats removed. The game starts and fatso goes into his coaching routine on the first play from scrimmage.

"See there! Tha's what I'm talkin' 'bout!" he bellows out. "Dooley's got Herschel runnin' straight ahead. Dumb! Jus' plain doggone dumb!"

"But he gained eighteen yards," I say, in defense of Dooley.

"Don't make no diff'rence. Oughta' run th' big dawg wide ever' time he ain't goin' out f'r a pass," he says.

This continues for the entire first half of the game, and everybody within ten yards of him hopes for a breather at half-time. No such luck. After refilling his tank, he takes up where he left off.

"Okay, now let me tell you what Dooley oughta'

do in th' second half. First, he oughta' surprise 'em with an inside kick. Then, put the big dawg at quarterback an'. . . ."

Everybody around him gets up and leaves. Everybody else knows why, except, of course, fatso.

I have the same luck in doctors' offices, restaurants, and airplanes. I no sooner take my seat than the guy next to me starts in.

"Would you like to hear about the years I spent in the Peace Corps?" he begins. And before I can say, "No thank you," he's off and running.

"Well, I first went to South America and . . . ." He will also get around to telling me how to curb inflation, cure the common cold, tune up a 1965 Mercury, and why the price of gold is so high.

If you listen long enough (which you won't), he'll explain the details of the O.J. Simpson trial, and why Jimmy Carter lost in 1980.

I guess the one that gets under my skin the most is the professional Yankee, the New Yorker who insists on going to war again the moment he hears my southern accent. And he's always either too little for me to beat up or too big for me to challenge.

It's almost always the same:

"Hey, fella'. Where you from?" he asks in a snide voice.

"Georgia."

"That right? I was down there once. In the Army, stationed at Fort Stewart. Know where that is?"

"Sure. It's near Hinesville, not far from Brunswick."

"Yeah, good old Highway 17. Hottest place I was ever in, 112 degrees in July."

"It gets pretty hot there all right."

"Do you'se guys still eat them grits down there?"

"Right. Almost every morning."

"I never could eat 'em. Tasted awful. I like Cream of Wheat myself."

"Well, I guess it's like the old man said when he kissed the cow, every man to his own choosin'," I said.

"I don't like the South. Just a bunch of little old two-bit towns and dirt farmer hicks. Ain't changed much since we whipped you'se guys in the Civil War, has it?"

"Well, you like the North and I like the South. Let's let it stand at that. Besides, I'm suffering from battle fatigue and too weary to talk about it or argue about it."

"Battle fatigue? Sorry about that fella'. Vietnam?"

"Nope."

"Korea?"

"Nope."

"World War II?"

"Nope. The Civil War."

"Aw, c'mon now. You're putting me on. The Civil War? That was some 130 years ago. How can you say you got battle fatigue from fighting in the Civil War?"

"I didn't say I got battle fatigue from fighting in the Civil War. I'm fatigued from talking and arguing about it with people like you."

SOUTHERNERS ON DISPLAY

MY TENURE IN NEW YORK CITY LASTED from April 1962 until August 1966. I fought battles reminiscent of the Civil War almost every day, winning some, losing some, and some were standoffs. I fought them in the office, at lunch, on commuter trains, during ball games, and—the bloodiest of them all—at office parties.

There were two of us from Georgia in the New York FBI office, Al Thomas from Shadydale, and myself, from Dublin. Almost without exception, the wife of a New York agent, after several cups of punch, would take another New York wife by the hand and seek one or both of us out.

"You have to hear these guys talk," she would say.

Al was pretty thin-skinned about any derogatory reference to his nativity, and at one Christmas party he let it show.

"Al, this is Gloria," the lead dog said. "She's never been down South. Say something southern for her."

It was like Al was on exhibition at a carnival sideshow and expected to perform on command. After six years of it he was fed up, and the latest request to perform was the straw that broke the camel's back.

Al hesitated for a moment, then looked his audience straight in the eye. He leaned forward a bit and said, "You wanna' hear somethin' southern, do ya'? All right, listen to this: 'Sheeeeit!' How was that, ma'am?" And with that, he walked away, not knowing that the female for whom he had performed was the boss's daughter.

There was also the repeated asking of "Where are you from?" to deal with. Al always answered, "Shadydale, Georgia," offering no clue as to where Shadydale was, leaving the questioner no more informed than before the question was asked.

I invariably got the same question, and after saying over and over that I was "from a little taown 'bout 150 miles south of Atlanter," I decided just to say, "I'm from Dublin, Georgia."

This led the unsuspecting Yankee snipers into my booby trap. Their next question was always, "Where is that?"

"Oh, it's just off Interstate 16, fifty miles east of Macon, on U.S. Highway 80 between 'Don't Litter' and 'Resume Speed,'" I would say, and walk away.

"Oh," the questioner could be heard to say, somewhat weakly. "Sure."

There was another agent from the South in the New York office, Al Whitfield. Well, Al wasn't really from the South. He was from Florida.

Al got his share of questions at the office parties, not about the way he talked but the name of his hometown—Wewahitchka. So he derived a spiel designed to leave not a shred of doubt as to his birthplace and how to get there.

"Ain't no problem, honey," he would say. "Comin' south from New York, when ya' hit th' mountains of north Georgia jus' keep on headin' south on whatever number road that road is 'til ya' git t' Hiawassee an' then turn right at Luke's Amoco. You go from Hiawassee to Ochlocknee to Talapoosa and through the Oochie Valley to Ellijay. In Ellijay, hang a left at Barfield's Pool Room, next to the Downtown Community All Faiths Church, an' stay on that same ol' road through Alapathee to Ludowici to Willacoochee to Attapulgus. Next you run smak dab into the entrance to the Okefenokee Swamp. (Be sure and go 'round that.) Stay on that same ol' road til' ya' cross th' Florida line. Go 'baout six miles an' you'll see Albert's Alligator and Snake Ranch. Don't do nothin' at Albert's. Jus' wave an' drive on by. Proceed nine miles to th' Tami Ami Trail and on to Waccassassa Bay. Smooth sailin' from there. Stay on that same ol' road to Umatilla, to Lecanto, to Homasassee, to Oklawaha, to Pahokee, to Appalachicola, to Lake Okeechobee. Turn right in Lake Okeechobee at Mrs. Duncan's Cafe and head south to Wewahitchka. When you see the city limits

sign, watch for the Wewahitchka fireplug. My house is the third one on the right past the fireplug. There's a pink plastic flamingo on the front lawn. You can't miss it."

Then, without another word, he would leave the party and go home, without a thought for his befuddled listener. A fella gets real tired of fighting such battles day and night, and, like so many years ago—losing. Would it help if I surrendered again? I doubt it.

WHAT YOU HEAR IS NOT WHAT YOU GET

ONE OF THE FIRST THINGS I NOTICED WHEN I moved north was that folks up there talk funny. Even little kids. It is very possible to mix and mingle for hours in a room with Yankees of all ages talking a mile a minute and have no idea what's being said, unless you have done your homework.

To help you should you ever visit the Big Apple, I have compiled a glossary that should prove invaluable. Naturally, the longer the visit, the more words you will need to add to the list. But for starters the

Revised and adapted from a story in Bo Whaley's *How to Love Yankees with a Clear Conscience* (Rutledge Hill Press, 1988)

words listed here should get one in and out the door and possibly help in avoiding embarrassment.

Under no circumstances should an innocent southern visitor make an attempt to repeat vocally what he hears while rubbing elbows "up yonder." It simply won't come out right and, besides, it is impossible to adapt to a foreign language on a short visit.

For your assistance and convenience, the Yankee spelling of each word is followed by the correct spelling of the word in parentheses. Also included is an example of how the word can be used in a sentence. These words are by no means a complete listing of the Yankee vocabulary, but rather key ones to have at your disposal.

Word	How It's Used
Gedouddaheah (*Get out of here*):	I'm fed up with your coming in late smelling of beer and cheap perfume. Just pack up your junk and gedouddaheah!
Whassamattayou (*What is the matter with you?*):	Loan you ten bucks when already ya'owe me twenty? Whassamattayou? Ya'crazy or somethin'?
Broad (*Woman; girl; female*):	Boy! Dat wuz some broad I seen ya' wit las' nite.
Fodder (*Father*):	Angelo says his Fodder can whip your Fodder.

Mudder *(Mother):* Oh, yeah? Dat may be, but I'll bet his Fodder can't whip my Mudder.

Goil *(Girl):* No doubt about it, Louie; dat Marie is da uglies' goil in P. S. 39. (P. S. 39 is a public school.)

Lorr *(Law):* My son, Herbie, was gonna go to Harvard an' study medicine but he changed his mind and went to Yale to study lorr.

Earl *(Oil):* Yeah, gimmee five bucks worth o' super unleaded an' check the earl.

Oil *(Earl):* Hey, Oil! While you're checkin' da earl how 'bout checkin' da batt'ry wadah.

BOIL with EARL

OIL with BERLE

True *(Through):* Are ya' believin' dis? Da traffic was so bad dis mornin' it took me more'n ten minutes ta' git true da' Lincoln Tunnel.

Tree *(Three):* Ya' say ya' wanna' git ta' where? Flatbush Avenue an' Roosevelt? No problem, go tree lights up an' turn right.

Wit *(With):* Jus' park your car, Dominick, an' you'se can ride wit me.

Hoi *(Hi!):* Hoi, gois! Are you'se goin' to da' poker game at Ricco's?

Goi *(Guy):* I seen dat play at da teeater las' nite, "Gois and Dolls." Great!

Erster *(Oyster):* Nah, can't make it to da union meetin' t'nite, Salvatore. Me'n Margie's going' over ta Hubuken (Hoboken) an' eat some ersters an' guzzle a few at th' Clam Broth House.

Boid *(Bird):* Dem Knicks don' stan' a chance. Da Celtics will eat 'em alive. Dat Larry Boid is da greates' dere is.

Joisey *(New Jersey):* Yeah, I work at Staten Island but I live ovah in Joisey (*Never* New Jersey).

Terlet *(Toilet):* Hello, Louie? Dis is Archie. Kin ya' git ovah ta my house right away? My terlet is stopped up.

Shoit *(Shirt):* Hey, Marie! What'd ya do wit my bowlin' shoit after ya ironed it?

Lawn Gyland
(Long Island):

Yea, Freddie, it's been good livin' in y'r neighborhood here in da Bronx, but me'n Hazel's movin' out. Bought us a place on Lawn Gyland.

Foist *(First):*

Hey! Whattayatalkin? My Gran'mudder can play foist base beddah dan dat bum!

Tanks *(Thanks):*

I'd rilly like ta go wit'cha to da races, Paul, but I made other plans a'ready. Tanks anyway.

Coib *(Curb):*

Can you imagine what dat stupid kid o' mine done? Took my car an' went speedin' down da Lawn Gyland Expressway an' jumped da coib. Hit a guy on a bicycle an' two joggers.

Fort *(Fourth):*

Know what Danny's teecher done? Da dumb broad flunked him an' now he's gotta' repeat da fort grade.

Toity-Toid
(Thirty-third):

Yeah, I been workin' out f'r th' las' tree munts at da Toity-Toid Street gym.

Trow *(Throw):*

I wuz talkin' ta Oinie's (Ernie's) pop las' nite an' he says da kid is gonna' sign wit da White Sox. Da kid kin rilly trow a baseball. Benny says he's been clocked at 98 miles per hour.

Single; Fin; Sawbuck; C-Note; Yard *($1; $5; $10; $100; $1,000):*

Hold it a minute, Jack, and let me step in the bank and get some change an' I'll put some green on ya. Two folks I always pay, my bookie an' da ol' lady's alimony. I need 12 singles, tree fins, a C-note, five sawbucks and four yards—$4,177. (Money Line: From what I gathered they have their own currency and money language in the Big Apple.)

Dis *(This):*

Well, I'll jus' tell you dis sport. Dis is a helluva' way ta run a railroad.

Dem *(Them):*

How da ya' like dem apples, huh?

Dat *(That):*

Ya can believe dis, George: Dat tie don' go wit dat suit.

Doze *(Those):*

It jus' ain't grammatically right ta say dem peoples, Sid. You s'pose ta say doze peoples.

Day *(They):*

Mama, I took da chicken soup to da Farenchello's house like you said, but day wasn't home.

Turteen *(Thirteen):*

I'll lay ya two ta one dat dere wasn't but turteen original states when America was created.

Tink *(Think):*

Well, I still tink dere was 14. How 'bout Brooklyn?

Taught *(Thought):*   I taught dere was 14, too, but Jimmy the bartender at Max's showed me a beer bottle what proved dere was jus' turteen.

Awriteareddy *(All right, already):*   Awriteareddy! I'm comin'! I'm comin'!

Den *(Then):*   O.K., Maria—first you cook the ground beef in a separate pan over medium heat. Den, you stir in the canned tomatoes and two pounds of garlic.

You'se *(You all):*   You'se guys wait till I git back an we'll go muggin' in Central Park.

Piece *(Gun):*   I never go near Central Park 'less I'm packin' my piece.

Duh *(The):* — Eddie, run down to duh deli an' tell Mr. Cohen to send me tree pounds of liverwurst.

Lotsa *(Lots of):* — I'd like a pepperoni and mushroom pizza, with lotsa mushrooms.

Donju *(Don't you):* — Donju leave this house till I get back!

Oily *(Early):* — I'm goin' ta Rosie an' Luigi's weddin' an' den stop by th' reception f'r a few minutes, but I have ta leave oily. Dis is da nite I watch rasslin' on TV, an' I don' miss that f'r nuttin'.

Witcha *(With you):* — Hey, Rocco! When you drive over ta Joisey t'morrer, can I go witcha?

Sawr *(Saw):* — I taut I sawr ya downta' Hoibie's dis mornin'.

Drawering *(Drawing):* — Hey, Marie! Whatcha drawerin' in dat colorin' book?

Potty *(Party):* — Can't make it, Joey. Me'n duh ol' lady is goin' to a Noo Yeer's Eve potty at Rafael's.

Doit *(Dirt):* — Trow a li'l doit in dat hole, Benjie, an' le's go tuh Angelo's f'r a beah.

Cuber *(Cuba):* — I tell youse whut I say; to hell wit Castro an' Cuber.

Avnoo *(Avenue):* — I'll meetcha' at Barney's on Flatbush Avnoo.

Moitle *(Myrtle):* Moitle an' Oil (Earl) is gittin' married at St. Luke's t'morrer.

Berld *(Boiled):* My ol' man says dat Khadafy oughta' be berld in earl.

Soitainly *(Certainly):* Whaddayatalkin? Soitainly I'm goin' tuh da Gients' game.

Champeen *(Champion):* I seen Joe Louis fight in duh Garden twice't when he was duh hevvyweight champeen.

Chiner *(China):* I wudeen take dat broad out in public f'r all duh tea in Chiner.

Consoined *(Concerned):* I'm consoined 'bout Oinie. He don' look right.

Emmer *(Emma):* I tell youse whut I tink. Dat Emmer Bombeck is a funny lady.

Poil *(Pearl):* Didja' hear 'bout dat bum, Oil? He found a poil in 'is erster.

Nize *(Noise):* Nah! I ain't buyin' no diesel cah. Makes too much nize.

Pok *(Park):* Seen duh papuh dis mornin'? Two more bums got dere's in Central Pok las' night.

Nuttin' *(Nothing):* Nuttin' doin', fella'. I ain't messin' wit no lottry.

Woids *(Words):* Ya' took duh woids right outta' my mout'.

Wantchas *(Want you):* I wantchas all tuh meet me in da Bronx brew'ry in da' mornin'.

Pitcher *(Picture):* Did'ja see dat pitcher o' Rombutello in duh *Times* dis mornin? Hard tuh reconize wit all dem bullet holes in 'is cheeks.

Choich *(Church):* I hoid dey foun' "Li'l" Joe behin' de choich ovah on Toity-Toid wit 'is neck broke.

Disere *(This here):* Wait a minute! Do it like disere.

Noospapuh *(Newspaper):* Yeah, I seen it in duh noospapuh.

Aintment *(Ointment):* Da skin ain't hardly broke. Jus' tell yer mommer tuh put a liddle aintment on it.

Cah *(Car):* Youse guys go on in an' git us a good seat while I pok duh cah.

Stiff *(Corpse):* Serves da stiff right fer gittin' caut in da ack. Dey's buryin' 'im dis afternoon in St. Bahneventure's.

Puss *(Face):* Frankie let 'im hol' one right in da puss an' laid 'im out col'.

Kisser (Same song, second verse).

Laig *(Leg):* Th' way I figgerit, he ain't got a laig tuh stand on. Guilty as sin, plus he's got hissef a crappy mout' piece.

Mout'piece *(Lawyer):* See above.

Joik *(Jerk):* Gedouddaheah! Da guy's a joik!

Bah *(Bar):*   Boy! Did I evah get smashed las' night! I stopped in at Bennie's Bah intent on havin' a couple, but I run inta' dat broad who's da featured strippah at Georgie's Strip n' Clip on Broadway an' we ended up at her place in Joisey. Wow! Fum dere it wuz light's out 'til dis mornin'.

Pleece *(Police):*   I seen da pleece cah wit duh lamp burnin' and duh wissel blowin' but I figgered it wuz jus' another cop late f'r lunch at Oscar's.

Dine *(Dying):*   Some train wreck las' night, huh? People dine all ovah duh place.

Figgah *(Figure):*   Did'ja see dat broad wit Kenny at duh fights las' night? Wow! Some figgah! Makes dat Dolly Parton look anemic, huh?

CHOWING DOWN AND STANDING IN LINE AT MAMA LEONE'S

MAMA LEONE'S IS UNDOUBTEDLY—IN MY humble opinion—the best Italian restaurant in New York City, if not the world. It was one of the plusses during my six-year stay in the city. While I make no pretense of being an authority on Italian food, I know what tastes good to me, and I had many enjoyable dinners at Mama Leone's.

Shortly after I began working in New York, a fellow FBI agent, Tony Masullo, invited me and my wife to have dinner with him and his wife at Mama Leone's. The food was great and the experience unforgettable. I had never before been to an authentic, garlic-smothered Italian restaurant. Neither had my wife. What we knew about Italian food was limited to an occasional plate of spaghetti for $3.50 at some high-school fund-raiser or church benefit back in Dublin.

Masullo had warned me that there would be a long line waiting to get in Mama Leone's, and he was right. I parked my car in the Madison Square Garden garage and had no sooner walked around the corner than I saw the line, and the Masullos. They were standing on the sidewalk, about fifty people from the entrance. My wife and I joined them, thereby becoming numbers fifty-one and fifty-two. Needless to say, numbers fifty-three and fifty-four weren't too happy about it. And they said so.

"There's always a line," said Masullo. "I've been in New York for twelve years now, and we eat here quite often. Always a line."

The food was worth the wait. When we parted company with the Masullos, I vowed to come back soon. I did, but a little sooner than I had anticipated. The New York FBI office, staffed with more than one thousand agents, had people transferring in and out almost every day. They came and went with the regularity of ants at a picnic.

I had only been in New York for a few weeks when a nice young agent, Ray Lamonica, transferred in from Birmingham. He and his wife, Pat, moved into my New Jersey neighborhood. Ray and I became quite close, as did our wives. We learned that Ray, a native of Buffalo, and Pat, a native of Syracuse, loved Italian food.

Inasmuch as I had been to Mama Leone's once, I assumed the role of an authority on the New York restaurant and invited Ray and Pat to go with me and my wife as our guests.

"I'd love to go," said Ray. "I've heard a lot about it but have never been."

We were set. We would go the next Saturday night, and I would drive.

We left right on schedule. It was raining, somewhere between a mist and a drizzle, just hard enough to keep the windshield wipers busy.

As we approached the Lincoln Tunnel, I said to Ray, who was seated up front with me, "There will be a long line when we get there. There's always a long line at Mama Leone's. It may take an hour or so to get seated."

"No problem," said Ray. "From what I've heard about the food the wait will be worth it."

"Oh, the food is great all right. The long line every night attests to that," I said as we exited the Lincoln Tunnel and headed for Madison Square Garden to park. "I always park in the Madison Square Garden parking garage when I go to Mama Leone's. Is that okay with you?"

"Fine with me. You're our leader. I know you won't steer us wrong," Ray said with confidence.

I pulled into the parking garage and checked the trunk of my car for an umbrella. No luck. I then remembered that I had left it in the office a few days before. I apologized.

As the four of us walked toward Mama Leone's, I again reminded Ray and Pat that they could expect a long line, and my prediction proved to be true. As we turned the corner, there it was. Probably seventy-five to one hundred people standing in line—in the rain that was now coming down a little harder. They were backed up against a building, and no one seemed to be talking with anyone else. Instead, they were all just staring straight ahead. The four of us joined them at the end of the line to begin our wait to enter Italian food heaven. The rain was cold.

We talked for a few minutes, never once noticing that the line wasn't moving. I waited for another five or six minutes and it still wasn't moving. Not even an inch. Being the designated leader of the group, I sensed an obligation to make an inquiry, although it didn't seem to make any difference to anyone else in line. They just stood still, like statues, and stared straight ahead. A few even tried to read their wet newspapers.

"I'll be right back," I said. "I'm gonna find out what the holdup is." With that I walked to the entrance to the restaurant and spoke to a man in a black and red uniform.

"Excuse me, sir. But I've been waiting for almost twenty minutes now and the line hasn't moved. Do you have any idea how long it will be before it starts moving?"

"Oh, I'd say about fifteen minutes. If the bus is on schedule."

"The bus? What bus?"

"The next bus to Queens. I'm waiting for it myself."

"You mean you aren't with Mama Leone's?"

"Nope. I'm with the Salvation Army. I just stepped down here to get out of the rain. We've been queued up here for about thirty minutes."

"Queued up?"

"Yeah, like I said. To catch the bus to Queens."

"You mean this is not the line waiting to get into Mama Leone's?"

"Nope, ain't no line tonight."

I walked back slowly to the end of the line, trying to come up with some sensible explanation.

"Find out anything?" asked Ray.

"Yes. There's no problem. We can go right in," I said with an air of importance.

"Gosh, that's great," said Pat. "I'm sure glad we came with you, you know, somebody who knows his way around the city and can get things done. But how in the world did you manage to get us in ahead of all those other people waiting in line?"

"Simple. Did you notice the man in the red and black uniform standing at the door?"

"Yes."

"Well, I just spoke to him and he told me to forget the line and go right in," I said, with just a whiff of nonchalance.

We had a great dinner; and when we walked back outside, the line was gone—to Queens.

SAINT PATRICK'S DAY—HERE AND THERE

I HADN'T BEEN IN NEW YORK SINCE MOVING back to Georgia from there in 1965, but in March 1978, I got the urge to return. I drove to Atlanta, boarded an airplane at 5:30 P.M., and in just over an hour I stepped off at LaGuardia Airport. It was Thursday, March 16. I wanted to spend St. Patrick's Day in the big city, see a Broadway play, and, above all, attend Mass at St. Patrick's Cathedral.

The play I saw while I was in the city, *Wiz*, was outstanding in the eyes of this amateur critic. But St. Patrick's was unforgettable. There was a special

Revised and adapted from a story in Bo Whaley's *How to Love Yankees with a Clear Conscience* (Rutledge Hill Press, 1988)

significance in worshiping there on St. Patrick's Day, March 17.

I paused momentarily at the door before entering to survey the setting of this legendary monument to Christianity. To my right, as I stood on the steps before the gigantic bronze doors, was yet another monument, this one to the fashion world—Sak's Fifth Avenue. To my left was Radio City Music Hall. Across the street, a bar loomed.

I looked upward, as do all tourists in New York, and gazed at the 330-foot spire pointing majestically toward heaven. Before entering St. Patrick's, I glanced back over my shoulder and took another look at the bar across the street.

Once inside, the bronze doors closed behind me and I was in another world. The rushing, buzzing, scurrying mass of humanity on Fifth Avenue that moments before had surrounded me was no longer in evidence. Though just thirty feet away, it was silent to those of us inside the cathedral.

I couldn't help but smile as I surveyed the spectacle that filled my eyes. St. Patrick's was outdrawing the bar across the street five hundred to one. I hoped God noticed it, too.

I treated myself to the beauty of the interior and greedily drank it in, becoming intoxicated on the beauty and serenity of it all. I wished my daddy could have been at my side, and although dead since 1969, maybe he was. He would have been pleased at the cathedral-bar ratio.

I seated myself near the rear and waited with more than 2,500 others for Mass to begin. I watched others enter and kneel. There was a man, impeccably dressed in a Chesterfield topcoat. He could easily have been chairman of the board at Chase Manhattan Bank. He was followed by a battered, wrinkled, and generally unkempt woman wearing a ragged, faded blue sweater. She could easily have been the charwoman who scrubbed the floors at Chase Manhattan. It made no difference. When the bronze doors closed behind them, the man and woman immediately became equals—at least for the next hour.

I watched them later, seated side by side, as the offering baskets were passed. I watched them drop their offerings in the basket, smiled, and comtemplated a familiar passage of Scripture, "The rich young ruler. . . . the widow's mite."

I listened intently as Father Charles Mahoney, perched high above the congregation, delivered his short sermon. It was impressive and satisfying to the soul. I was proud to be a Christian and part of it all.

When Father Mahoney finished his sermon, I watched as the hundreds strolled forward to the altar to receive Holy Communion. The "banker" and the "charwoman" walked down the long aisle together—and back—as equals.

It was beautiful.

BAR TALK

IF YOU ARE A STRANGER IN A NEW YORK neighborhood bar, not only do you have the right under the Miranda Warning to remain silent but you have an obligation under the threat of being beat about the head and shoulders to remain silent. The regulars, including the bartender, ain't really interested in nothing you have to say—but there are those who refuse to abide by the rules and spout off at the mouth in a vain attempt at comedy.

In New York, neighborhood bars are sacred territory. It's where hard-working men let off steam, exchange stories, and analyze professional sports, especially football. There are three things close to a man's heart in New York—his home, his job, and his bar. It doesn't pay for an outsider to mess with any of them.

Late one afternoon a sickly looking little fellow weighing about 130 pounds, wearing horn-rimmed glasses, a pink sweater, and saddle oxfords strolled into a neighborhood bar in the Bronx. The bartender, a burly fellow, and three customers were there, seated at the bar drinking beer. The little fella ordered a Pina Colada. That raised eyebrows.

"Heavy on the pineapple juice," he said.

Halfway into his drink he asked the bartender, "Wanna' hear a good joke?' "

The bartender merely shrugged his shoulders and continued wiping beer mugs.

"It's about a football player," the little fellow said, and with this the three customers shifted on their barstools to look in his direction and listen.

"Well, this football player at Notre Dame was all excited as he told one of his teammates that he had become engaged to a cheerleader and was going to give her an engagement ring that night. He reached in his pocket and pulled out a ring with a large stone to show him.

"Boy! That's a beauty!" his teammate commented. "How big is that stone?"

"Three carats," he said proudly.

"Three carats? Wow! Is it a real diamond?'

"It better be. If it ain't, then I've been cheated out of fourteen dollars and seventy-five cents!"

The bartender never changed his expression, or said a word. Neither did the three customers, all as big as Paul Bunyan.

Sensing that the bartender hadn't understood the punch line, the little fella explained it to him. Still no change of expression. He merely mumbled, leaned over the bar, and looked the little guy right in the eyes.

"Son, where you from?" asked the bartender.

"Hardeeville, South Carolina," he answered proudly.

"Well, you see that big fella sitting at the end of the bar?"

"Right. The one with the big nose?"

"Do you know who he is?"

"Nope, 'fraid not."

"He's the middle linebacker for the New York Giants. Now then, see the big fella at the other end? He plays defensive end for the New York Jets and was captain of the Notre Dame football team two years ago. And the big, tough looking guy sitting there next to the beer dispenser? That's 'Mean Joe' Greene of the Pittsburgh Steelers. Now, would you like to tell that joke again, and speak up, so they can hear it?"

The little fella studied for a minute, slid down off his barstool, and turned to walk out, saying, "Naw. I don't think so."

"What's the matter, you chicken or something?"

"Oh, no. It's not that."

"Then why don't you tell them your joke?"

"Well, it's like this," the little fella said, "I just don't want to have to explain it three more times."

We didn't have neighborhood bars down in south Georgia where I grew up. We didn't even really

have neighborhoods—or bars. That's not to say that booze wasn't in plentiful supply, because it was.

Ol' man George Butler sold gallons of it every Saturday night from the back door of his store. Not much business came in the front door, but a heck of a lot went out the back.

Ned Bristol owned a gasoline station and sold gallon on top of gallon on Sunday mornings. Liquor, not gasoline. He made it during the week and sold it on Sunday, but no sales between 9:30 A.M. and noon. Ol' Ned was a religious man, and he refused to do business during Sunday school and church. When a regular customer—and they were all regular customers of long standing—said to Ned, "Lemmee have two gallons," Ned didn't head for the gasoline pump but to the hayloft in his barn, where he kept his merchandise stored. The sheriff once said, "Ol' Ned's got a thirty-five-dollar barn with ten thousand dollars' worth of corn likker in the hayloft."

And Ned's neighbor, Ralph Hall, swears to this day that one Saturday when Ned and his wife had the preacher over for dinner, Ned made a mistake. Ned's wife was an excellent cook and the preacher was a hearty eater who loved fresh vegetables. When he said to Ned, "Brother Bristol, I believe I'd like some more of that wonderful and tasty corn," Ned responded in a flash. "Yessir, Preacher," he said. "Jus' pass me y'r glass an' I'll pour it f'r ya'." Needless to say, the preacher and his wife did not stay for dessert.

No Honor Among the Homefolks

And Jesus said unto them, "A prophet is not without honour, save in his own country, and in his own house." Matthew 13:57.

And in his hometown, too . . .

There are those who feel that success in any degree is ample reason for all who know him to respect and honor him. But this isn't always the case. Royce Atkins, who grew up in a small town in South Carolina, learned this firsthand.

Royce attended high school in his hometown and was an excellent student. Although his graduating class was small, just nineteen students, he was the valedictorian and class president. His excellent scholastic record earned him a scholarship to the University of South Carolina in Columbia, where he majored in economics and also finished with an excellent scholastic record, ranking third in his class.

After graduation New York beckoned and he answered the call of a highly successful and well-known bank, going to work as a trainee in the trust department. Royce did well, received periodic promotions on schedule, and in eight years was a bank vice president. After thirteen years he was executive vice president in charge of the trust department.

Royce became well known in banking circles in New York, was a member of several prestigious business and social clubs, and lived in a fine Manhattan apartment. He drove a very expensive luxury automobile, wore Brooks Brothers suits, and had his shirts custom made. New York was his oyster.

As the years went by, Royce continued to progress, and eventually he became first vice president in charge of bank operations, second from the top. Then, after twenty-eight years with the bank, he was named president and chief operating officer.

Royce had become a wealthy man. At the age of fifty-one, he had never married. He also had not visited his hometown since leaving some twenty-eight years before, opting to fly his mother and father to New York for periodic visits.

Then, one night, he received a telephone call from his mother. "Royce, your daddy is mighty sick. The doctor says he's had a stroke. If you can get away I know your daddy would like to see you."

"I'll be there as quick as I can, Mama," he said. "Please tell Daddy that."

The next morning Royce flew out of New York's LaGuardia Airport to Columbia, South Carolina. From there, he was able to take a taxi to his parents' house.

As the cab driver made his way toward Royce's neighborhood, Royce began to reminisce. Coogle's Gas Station was still there, but it had new pumps and a convenience store had been added. The Methodist Church needed a paint job. It needed one when he left almost thirty years before. The old courthouse, with old men sitting on the steps, was still the largest building in town. The clock was still broken. He looked at his watch—2:25 P.M., although the courthouse clock indicated that it was 9:18.

The taxi passed the school from which he had graduated, and the gymnasium in back where he played basketball inside and would sneak outside for a cigarette with a few of his cronies behind it. He also thought about his first kiss, his first real kiss, from Miriam Buckley. It happened behind the gymnasium when he was in the eighth grade. He wondered where she was now.

Old man Border's hardware store was empty, the front window boarded up with graffiti sprayed all over it. What a shame, he thought.

Royce asked the cab driver to stop at the local market. Royce would get a Coke and walk the last three blocks, taking the opportunity to collect himself for what lay ahead.

He walked inside the store with his raincoat over his arm, an overnight bag in his right hand, and his briefcase in his left. Inside, he went to the restroom to freshen up and comb his hair.

Upon leaving the store, he soon realized that he had left his raincoat at the market. He entered the front door and immediately saw a familiar face coming toward him. It was Booker, who had been employed at the store, in a variety of positions, for as long as Royce could remember. He concluded that Booker had to be at least eighty, maybe more.

"Hello, Booker!" Royce greeted him as they met.

"Oh, hello Mr. Royce," Booker said. "You goin' outta town?"

Royce, the prophet, had just had Matthew 13:57 verified.

Preconceived
Notions

Here are some wrong ideas northern-
ers have about all of us living south of the youse
guys-y'all dividing line. These ideas hold up to
scrutiny about as well as some of those that southerners have about Yankees.

- Southerners talk funnier than they do.

- All women in the South are in the kitchen, bare
  foot and pregnant. Not anymore. Some spend a
  lot of time in the den.

- Moonshine is the regional drink and is served
  at all wedding receptions. This can't be true. If
  it were, the groom would never be able to back

out of the driveway and get on with the honey-moon.

- The majority of southern men spend most of their time hunting and fishing. I don't know a lot about that, other than it takes almost as much time to scale fish and clean birds as it does to catch 'em and kill 'em.

- All southern girls fourteen years of age and over are married. Nonsense. I know a bunch in that age category who just shack up.

- Grits grow on trees.

- There really ain't no such thing as buttermilk. Sure there is! It comes from a butter cow, and if your stomach looks anything like the glass it is downed from after it dries, then heaven help you!

- "Dixie" is sung at all weddings and funerals.

- Southerners eat clabber as a substitute for yo-gurt.

- Mules are extinct.

- Jack Daniel invented whiskey.

- Hardly anybody down South watches the *Late Show with David Letterman*. Well, more people would watch it if it wasn't on opposite the *Soy bean Report* and *How to Whittle While the Mash Ferments*.

- Sunday afternoons are spent sitting under a giant magnolia tree, drinking mint juleps. Most southerners outside of Louisville, Kentucky, ain't never seen a mint julep, and most of the giant magnolias have long since been cut for pulpwood.

- A man has two prized possessions—his bird dog and his wife—and prays long and hard that he'll never have to make a choice between them. While he can always stick something frozen in the microwave, it's pretty hard to find a wife who'll hold a point or retrieve quail.

I'm sure you could come up with some misconceptions of your own. Let me know.

WHEN A WAVE IS AS GOOD AS A HOWDY

IT DIDN'T TAKE ME LONG TO REALIZE THAT communicating with New Yorkers ain't really the easiest thing in the world to do. You can speak to 'em on the street and they never indicate they heard you, with the exception of a few ladies of the night— and day—who parade regularly in the area of Times Square. Speak to one of 'em and she'll be all over you like a cheap suit.

Down where I come from everybody speaks to everybody else as a matter of habit and proper up-bringing, and everybody you speak to returns the greeting. We call it being neighborly. You do that in New York and whoever you speak to figures right off that you want something.

There are times down home when it ain't convenient to speak, like at the high school championship basketball game in a gymnasium full of yelling maniacs, in the library where talking is a no-no, in church where you figure Jesus is listening, at a University of Georgia football game immediately following a Bulldog touchdown, or at a benefit "all-you-can-eat catfish supper for $4.00" because everybody usually has their mouths full. In these circumstances a wave is as good as a howdy. Just raise either hand and the intended recipient will acknowledge with either a return wave or a nod of the head.

Should you wave at somebody and he refuses to return your gesture of cordiality, you immediately characterize him as "snooty" and go about your business. Once in a while he will call later to explain why he wasn't in a position to wave back. Such explanations are readily acceptable and the caller is immediately reinstated with full privileges in the wavers' club.

Waving is automatic in the Southland, with never a second thought as to whether to wave or not. We wave everywhere—on the sidewalk, while driving our pickups, on the porch, sitting in front of the courthouse, almost anywhere. We also wave at everybody, whether we know them or not. That is not a consideration. We wave at prisoners working on the side of the road, little children and senior citizens, pretty young girls and ugly old men, the rich and the poor, politicians and preachers, and bus drivers—it makes no difference to us. Everybody gets waved at sometime during the day, and most more than once.

There are times, however, when it isn't convenient to wave and no wave is expected. Here are a few such situations:

When someone waves at an individual in his garden and he has an armload of just pulled corn, he is not expected to wave back. However, a gentle nod to the waver to verify that his wave is acknowledged is appreciated.

When the mail carrier sticks the mail in a mailbox and sees no one around, he usually blows his horn to notify the individuals inside the house that he has placed mail in their mailbox. This is regarded as a substitute audible wave for those who couldn't see a visible one.

It is not necessary to return a wave to a passerby when seated in a rocking chair on your front porch shelling peas or butterbeans. A smile or a nod will suffice. (For the benefit of New Yorkers, a front porch is a covered entrance to a house, usually projecting from the wall and having a separate roof. It is a favorite place for meditation and rest, along with a midday snooze. The affluent call it a verandah. At The White House it is called a portico, except when Jimmy Carter was president and it was referred to by the Carter clan as a "porchico," with the South Porchico being the best known.)

If by chance you see someone approaching that you don't care to speak to or wave at, simply stop, bend over, and pretend to tie your shoe. Keep your eyes pointed downward until the threat has passed.

In the vast majority of cases people who are waved to in the South wave back. It is an accepted means of communication that has been utilized by the sons and daughters of the South for many decades. Some of them probably waved at Sherman as he burned his way to the sea.

There is no discrimination in waving. Men wave at women, women wave at men, boys wave at girls, girls wave at boys. An innocent wave has many times led to a lasting relationship—or at least a meaningful one-night stand.

One of the more popular and often employed waves is the mini-wave. It is the wave of choice by most people when driving. Here's how it works:

When meeting an oncoming vehicle simply lift your right forefinger off the top of the steering wheel and wiggle it slightly for the driver to see. Or, when you pass someone who is walking and doesn't see you coming, use the same forefinger procedure along with a short toot of your horn. In almost all cases your mini-wave will attract a return wave.

I once had a discussion with a fellow FBI agent in New York regarding the mini-wave. He was a native New Yorker (Brooklyn, Bedford-Stuyvesant section) and loyal to his roots. I appreciated that in him.

"You'se guys are always sayin' dat Noo Yarkers don't respond to y'r finger wave, when ya' wiggle dat fingah at oncoming drivahs," he said, as we drove along Riverside Drive in Manhattan. "Well, I tell ya'—dat's a bunch o'bloney. Noo Yarkers is jus' as freely as you'se guys from da' Sout are, sometime mebbe morrh."

I was driving and suggested that we survey the next ten cars we met. I would give them the forefinger wiggle and see if I got a return.

"Yeah? You're on, fella'. You wiggle 'em an' I'll watch 'em. Okay?"

"Okay."

I employed the forefinger wiggle at the next ten drivers.

"Arright! Ya' see dare? Eight outta' ten give it back to ya', and dem uddah two mebbe didn' see ya', huh?"

He was right, but he overlooked one thing of prime importance—New Yorkers use a different finger.

WHAT I MISS ABOUT NEW YORK

- Bronx Zoo
- Central Park
- Coney Island hot dogs
- Great plays on Broadway (and some off Broadway)
- Greenwich Village
- Italian food
- New Year's Eve in Times Square
- New York skyline at night
- Rockettes at Radio City Music Hall
- Saint Patrick's Cathedral
- Sale days at Macy's
- Sunday afternoon baseball with the Yankees

WHAT I DON'T MISS ABOUT NEW YORK

- Accents
- Central Park
- Commuting
- Crowded subways
- High taxes
- Honking taxis
- Litter
- Long lines
- People urinating in the streets
- Rude clerks
- Rush hour
- Sirens

HEY YOU! HERE'S YOUR CHANCE TO BE THE REDNECK YOU ALWAYS DREAMED OF!

At absolutely no cost, you can become a member of the Redneck Society of America and, therefore, be a certified, bonafide redneck. We'll even send you a certificate to prove it! It's a good-lookin' thang, suitable for framin' and displayin'. And, best of all, it's FREE! Just imagine livin' the life of a redneck and practicin' all that's entitled to you—swimmin' in the creek nekkid, chewin' tooth-picks by the box, and shootin' holes in road signs, just to name a few. You already do all those things, you say? Great! Now you have the chance to make it official and impress your friends to boot.

To receive your FREE credential of redneck-ness, write to Certify Me Red, Rutledge Hill Press, 211 Seventh Avenue North, Nashville, TN 37219-1823 and let us know you're ready to accept your God-given title of "certified, bonafide redneck"!

The Redneck Society of America
Hee Haw, Georgia

∞ This Certifies That ∞

_____

has demonstrated all the necessary requirements for membership in The Redneck Society of America and is therefore received into the society with all the rights, honors, and privileges appertaining thereunto. Thusfore, as a certified, bonafide redneck, the above noted is entitled to chew tobacco, eat grits, hunt possums, go bare-footed, smoke Salem Light 100's, drive an El Camino, swim in the creek nekkid, chew toothpicks by the box, drink buttermilk, call your grandparents Mee-Maw and Paw-Paw, have big hair, watch fishing shows on the cable, wear a belt with your name on the back, have more cars in your front yard than in your driveway, marry any-body under the age of thirteen but no closer kin than a double first cousin or a second cousin once removed, eat Velveeta, hang Elvis pictures in the double-wide and a gun-rack in every vehicle you own, wear tube tops, own a satellite dish larger than your home, name your children after race car drivers, put the washin' machine on the front porch and a pink plastic flamingo in the front yard, put peanuts in your Coke, wear offensive T-shirts, have a tattoo of your first love on a body part, wear a ring on each finger and stand with your hand over your heart every time you hear "Freebird."

In witness whereof, the undersigned has affixed his/her name and the official seal of

The Redneck Society of America on this _____ day

of _____ in the year of our Lord _____.

Bo Whaley, Certified Redneck and President of The Redneck Society of America

Bo Whaley has won twenty-one awards as a columnist for the Dublin, Georgia, *Courier Herald*. He
speaks to more than two hundred audiences each
year, hosts a morning radio talk show, is the author
of *Rednecks and Other Bonafide Americans*, and "loafs
a lot."